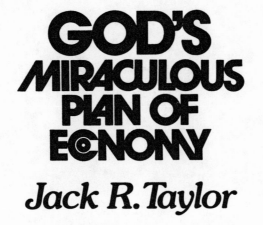

GOD'S MIRACULOUS PLAN OF ECONOMY

Jack R. Taylor

Broadman Press/Nashville, Tennessee

Scripture quotations marked NEB in parentheses are from *The New English Bible* © The Delegates of the Oxford University Press and The Syndics of the Cambridge University Press, 1961, 1970. Reprinted by permission.

Scripture quotations marked TLB in parentheses are from *The Living Bible, Paraphrased* (Wheaton: Tyndale House Publishers, 1971) and are used by permission.

Dewey Decimal Classification: 248.6
Subject Headings: STEWARDSHIP/FINANCE, PERSONAL
Library of Congress Catalog Card Number: 75-27411
Printed in the United States of America

ACKNOWLEDGMENTS

To my wife, *Barbara*, daughter, *Tammy*, and son, *Timmy*, whose lives have been a part of the exciting laboratory in which the principles of this volume began to first be proved in our lives. Family, you have been incomparable.

To my *Mom* and *Dad* whose support and esteem have been like shouts of encouragement from the grandstands. Thanks, Mom and Dad!

To *Manley Beasley* whose preaching on faith first urged me to step out on God's principles of economy. Friend, the adventure has been exciting!

To *Bill Stafford* whose concepts on economy have been of further help in my own life and ministry, and from whom many of the principles herein were drawn. Friend, your life has helped me!

To the *Castle Hills Baptist Church* which served as a proving ground for the working out of these principles. Thanks to those who were part of the journey.

To all those who have never been free from the pressure of an economy where there has never been quite enough . . . WELCOME . . . to the world of God's plenty in every realm!

JACK R. TAYLOR

FOREWORD

One of the great delights of my ministry is to raise money for the Kingdom. Without apology my philosophy has always been: if a project is worth receiving an offering for, it is worth going after all you can get! In my judgment, the greatest thing I can do for a man is to tell him how to be saved; the second greatest thing I can do for him is to tell him how to be filled and how to walk in the Spirit; and the third . . . how to be rightly related to God with his money.

Through the years I have approached the matter of stewardship from a number of perspectives. Recently there came to my attention a concept of giving in a sermon by Jack Taylor. I was so fascinated and captivated about what I heard that I preached it word-for-word to our Sunday morning congregation. Our people, through the years, have been trained to give through the Sunday School. Our morning plate offering, therefore, is usually only about $200. On this particular Sunday morning we received the usual Sunday morning offering at the end of the sermon. The result . . . $22,650 in the plate, plus the usual $20,000 through the Sunday School.

I have captured the philosophy of Jack Taylor's thesis regarding Christian stewardship embodied in these pages and have preached it about a dozen times to different congregations. The result—always the same! What a pity it is that in these days of so-called "tight money," most churches in Christian causes are retreating when, as Jack so eloquently says, "My Heavenly Father owns all the wealth in this world and in the world to come." David said, "I am old and have been young, but I have never seen the righteous forsaken or his seed begging bread."

Today is the greatest opportunity for missionary advance in the history of the world. Most believers seem to think that God is broke! There is plenty of money—more than there has ever been, and God owns it, circulating for his cause. This book will tell you how to make that happen in your own life and ministry. We are no beggar's children, and He has more than enough to finance His work. The budget of our own church has grown in the last five years from one-third of a million dollars to over one million dollars annually, and all the while, numbers of our people are becoming very financially prosperous. The reason? We have found the principles that Mr. Taylor teaches, and are practicing them. The price you pay for this book will probably be the best investment you have ever made in your life!

JOHN R. BISAGNO
First Baptist Church
Houston, Texas

CONTENTS

And God is able to make all grace
abound toward you; that ye, always
having all sufficiency in all things,
may abound to every good work.
                    2 Corinthians 9:8

INTRODUCTION

Pick up a Bible. Any Bible will do. Now hold it up before your eyes. You are holding in your hand a miracle Book! Three miracles distinguish it from all the books of the world and defend it against ordinariness.

There is, first, the miracle of INSPIRATION: *that work of the Spirit of God in the hearts and minds of the Scripture writers which made their writings a record of divine revelation.* That book is God-breathed! From its inception it was divine. In it is the mind of God, the way of salvation, and the revealed plan of God for man for time and eternity. It is divine in its *initiation*.

There is, second, the miracle of PRESERVATION: *that work of the Spirit of God upon the hearts, minds, and hands of the Scripture translators, as well as upon the Scripture text itself, which guaranteed the perpetuation and protection of the original message of the Bible.* Through the perils of translation and re-translation, changing times and cultures, the same Holy Spirit who breathed the original message to the first writers has been present to protect the text against deceit and error. So miraculously did the Holy Spirit work that the Bible has retained its impact and intent through hundreds of perilous years of translation. God did not leave the care of his Word to the hands of men alone. It is divine in its *continuation*.

There is, finally, the miracle of ILLUMINATION: *that work of the Spirit of God upon the heart, mind, and life of the preacher,*

9

the teacher, and the student of the Word which discloses the inner meaning of the message of the Bible. No little miracle this! The same Holy Spirit which breathed the Word into the hearts of the writers and presided over its perpetuation now moves upon the preacher, teacher, and student to reveal its life-changing truths. It is divine in its *communication.*

Thus, you have physical, tangible, visible proof of the existence of miracles. You are holding a miracle in your hand! The Bible is miraculous in its *initiation,* in its *continuation,* and in its *illumination.* The Holy Spirit still guards his Word! If you doubt its miraculous nature, I challenge you to give the Holy Spirit an opportunity to speak to your heart through its contents as you read it. God's eternal disposition regarding his Word is revealed in Jeremiah 1:12: "I will hasten my word to perform it!"

In this Book, the mind and plan of God are disclosed. It contains the plan of life for all men and all seasons and is eternal, unchanging, and complete . . . from eternity to eternity.

The systems of man are collapsing and passing into antiquity. This should be no surprise to us. We have read the divine utterance which says, "And the world is passing away with its desires; but he that does the will of God abides forever" (1 John 2:17).

The Bible presents the rules of *eternal* life. Its principles dare to cut clean across the lines of modern reason, defy the best of our system's experts, and extol values long since claimed obsolete by this world's intelligentsia. The Bible claims things to be precious that the world abhors and abhors things which this world holds precious.

And the remarkable thing about all this is that the world's claims make so much sense to the reasoning mind and the Bible seems to make so little. In the thinking of the world, the Bible seems preposterous and absurd . . . its claims far-out! I cannot argue this. But with as much sense as the deductions of the world seem to be making, they are not working! The world is falling apart, and its systems are failing! Man is scrambling to patch up his plans but they are passing away, despite it all. They simply are not working.

But I can tell you this . . . I affirm that the claims of the Bible *are* working! Right at this moment they are working! In the lives of men and women who dare to demonstrate their faith in the trustworthiness of the Word of God, heaven is happening! It is working! Its claims, as absurd as they sound, are standing. So I give you this Book, the Bible . . . laughed at, challenged, doubted, scoffed at, opposed, and refused . . . but whose principles stand!

Now we come to the reason for this volume. The Bible is a completely reliable Book which presents the history of man from a divine perspective and proposes a management of man's affairs under a plan of divine economy.

Thus, there is a plan of economy which is eternal. It is a plan for all men and all seasons, and it involves all the commodities of life. That plan of economy is the will of God. G. Campbell Morgan said, "The one and only life that sets a man free from the forces that blight and destroy is the WILL OF GOD. Show me a man who lives for one day wholly, utterly, in word and thought and deed in the will of God, and I will show you a man who is antedating heaven, and who for that day reaches the plane of life which is at once broadest, freest, and gladdest."

The Word of God is given us that we might know the truth . . . not that we might have another theory with which to compare already existing ideas. The truth that the Bible reveals is the will of God.

The plan of economy presented in the Bible is stable and workable. It will work in good times and bad among people of all classes and races, young and old. It will still be in effect when the stars begin to fall, and a hundred million years from this very moment will still be standing. Such a plan deserves the consideration of every reasoning person today.

In these days when every magazine, newspaper, and television

newscast is headlining the present economic disaster around the
world and heralding the possibility of the collapse of the whole
economic system, surely it is time to view the plan of economy
that was in force when civilization saw its first sunrise and will
be in force after the last sunset!

There is a plan of economy presented in the Bible which is
not affected by recession, depression, spiraling inflation and dollar
devaluation. It is God's plan! It involves the management of all
the affairs of man in this world and all the commodities of life.
This is not a volume about money alone, because economy involves much more than money. It includes all the products with
which man deals during his life—and after. A plan of economy
that does not include the view of eternity is indeed incomplete!
This plan takes into account time and eternity. It reckons with
all earth's treasures, resources, and capacities and man's role
in relating himself to them. It includes the eternal purpose in
the mind of God as he created all that is.

Man's economic systems are collapsing because he has been
selfish and shortsighted and has failed to include in his economic
principles those matters vital to its permanency. He has not
reckoned with his responsibilities to the God who made all things,
as well as himself, nor has he reckoned with his relationship
with the whole human family. He has trafficked to his immediate
advantage with divinely-given privileges, and the result has been
the destruction of resources necessary to the whole human family.

The price for man's crimes is high. The whole balance of
economy is out of order. There is too much here and not enough
there. Greed reigns, and war rages. The confusion and consterna-
tion among nations are but a magnification of what is going on
in the hearts of men. The "evil day" has always come when the
deceit of man's systems has finally cornered him . . . when his
violations of divine rules of economy have finally apprehended
him. That day is near again! When it came the nation fell, the
enemy took over, the famine came, the siege was executed . . .
and whatever else happened that needed to happen to remind

people that God was still in charge and demanded attention.

Long-standing rules on which we have based our world economy have at long last proved invalid. Shortages in all commodities are threatening. For the first time man can remember, famine is conceivable in every part of the world.

Surely it is high time to ask, "Does the God of heaven have anything to say to this turbulent, torn-up twentieth century?" Of course he does! He has always had something to say, and he has always been saying it for those who listen. He does have a plan for your life! It is all-inclusive of every relationship, commodity, capacity now and later. It embraces what you are and all you will ever be. It includes your time, your concern, your love, your emotional and mental capacities, and your spiritual gifts.

It is God's miraculous plan of economy. Miraculous? Certainly! Because it is God's plan and because its workings cannot be explained by the rules of earth. The prayer of the author is that the reader will find it impossible to respond with a casual shrug of the shoulders to the message of this volume. I pray that it will result in whatever changes in the reader's life-style are necessary to adjust him into God's plan of economy. I pray that the message of this book will endanger and imperil any life-style which disregards the will of God as man's supreme goal and cause an encounter which will result in your getting in on God's way of doing things!

May the principles herein be as life-changing for you as they are proving to be for me!

JACK R. TAYLOR

1
THREE GREAT, GRAVE QUESTIONS

The manner in which we answer certain key questions will determine for us the outcome of the whole matter. Our actions regarding an issue may be perfectly consistent with our conclusions, but if those conclusions are faulty such consistency is futile. Thus, it is vital that we answer at least three questions:

WHAT IS REALITY?
WHY ARE WE HERE?
WHAT IS GOD UP TO?

These are great questions, because they are universal in their influence; grave, because unless we find the right answers and make proper application of the answers, our lives will be greatly hampered in reaching their full and intended meaning.

If our answers to these questions are incorrect, we shall miss God's plan of economy even though those answers may reflect agreement with this world's opinions. Let's study those answers.

WHAT IS REALITY?

The Christian lives in two realms or dimensions . . . the spiritual and the physical, or to put it another way, visible and invisible; or still another way, tangible and intangible. His ability to put those two realms in proper perspective with each other determines whether or not he succeeds as a Christian.

The world would answer the question of reality's substance by saying, "That's simple . . . reality is what you can see, touch, taste, smell, and hear." This is exactly what we are prone to believe on the basis of what we know as mere human beings. And it sounds so sensible and logical! "This is real!" I exclaim as I pound on the table beside my typewriter. "This is real!" I declare as I hold up a book which I have been reading. And few would dare to disagree with such a fundamental claim supported by the senses. Our conclusion, if not contested, will be that the obvious is reality, and the unobvious is non-reality. It is not difficult to see where that leaves the Christian seeking to live with eternity in view. He is consigned to live out his life in terms of the world's definition of reality, and this completely cripples him for the dimension of the spiritual.

Now, are you ready for what God says about reality? Here it is:

"Meanwhile our eyes are fixed, not on things that are seen, but on things that are unseen: for what is seen passes away; what is unseen is eternal" (2 Cor. 4:18, NEB).

Which is the more real, that which is temporary or that which is permanent? The permanent, of course! Here the Word of God tells us that those things which are seen are passing away. The King James Version says, "For the things which are seen are temporal." The word for *temporal* is interesting. It is a combination of two Greek words, *kairos*, meaning "for a while, a season, or a time," and *pros*, a preposition meaning "toward or pertaining to." Thus, you have the total implication of the statement, "The things that are seen pertain to a season."

Thus, we have done away with man's idea of the definition of reality. We now know what is *not* reality. *That which is seen is not ultimate reality.* It is not deserving of our final trust. It is passing away. We cannot rest our values on that which is seen. It is unsound economy to have our trust placed in what our eyes can see and our hands can touch.

That is real which lasts. Look around you. You cannot see anything that lasts. Your hands cannot hold anything that lasts. That which is seen in passing. What is unseen is eternal! This simply means that the only dimension that we can trust is the spiritual dimension. Yet, the response of many believers is, "Let's not deal in the vague things of the unseen . . . I want something practical!" What they are saying is that they want something that can be confirmed by their senses. The Bible tells us that we have received the Spirit of God that we might *know* the things that are freely given us of God (1 Cor. 2:12). We are then informed that the natural man receives not the things of the Spirit of God for they are foolishness to him. He cannot know them, for they are spiritually discerned. While senses can discern the "seen," only spirit can discern the spiritual.

Now, the answer . . . that only is ultimate reality which is spiritual. When I meet you, I see a combination of the temporal and the eternal. Your body is temporal and is passing away. You are spirit and are eternal. You will still be around a million years from today! Your body as it is now will have long since ceased to exist. You will have a new body which will be of eternal substance.

If we are to know and practice God's plan of economy, we must settle this matter of the identity of reality and rest upon it. If we waver from our conclusion that reality is spirit, we shall find ourselves in continual confusion and ceaseless chaos.

Let us state this truth from another direction. God is the ground of all that is, the source of all reality. Man's trouble is that with the crippling conclusion that reality is what we see . . . God has no place in his thinking. Since God is the source of all reality and God is Spirit, then the basic makeup of reality is spiritual. We must believe that! I want to give you a verse that we will be dealing with in an extensive fashion later, but which is appropriate here:

"Source, Guide, and Goal of all that is—to him be glory forever" (Rom. 11:36, NEB).

"For of him, and through him, and to him, are all things: to whom be glory for ever, amen" (Rom. 11:36, KJV)!

There you have it! Everything comes *from* him, everything goes *to* him, and everything exists *through* him! He is all in all!

Now this does not depreciate the value of the things which are seen. Rather, it places them in their highest position in perspective with their spiritual counterparts. If God is the ground of all that is, then all that we see is merely a visible counterpart of an invisible reality. We get a hint of this as Paul says, "For the invisible things of him from the creation of the world are clearly seen, being understood by the things that are made, even his eternal power and Godhead" (Rom. 1:20). This makes the true value of what our eyes can see rest upon our seeing through them to the invisible things of him. These things serve as windows through which to see the real. "Being understood by the things that are made"—Rom. 1:20. Thus, we can rightly say that the Christian is one who has the ability to see through the *obvious* to the *actual*.

Thus, God is Reality! He is the main reality. All that we see in the universe is a reflection of God's handiwork. *Of him, through him, and to him are all things.* Any solid, stable economy must rest on that triad. Everything must be viewed through that perspective. That means that our plan of economy must have the "God point of view." The value of anything must be measured in the light of that view.

This is foundational! Please believe this! If your reality is confined to an economy which rests on your bank account, your house, your cars, your human resources, then you have no foundation for proceeding into God's plan. If God is all in all and is more real to you and me than our physical resources, then we shall never lack! Everything we see will simply be a challenge to "see through to him." Let me illustrate this. Think of a present need you are experiencing. If you have a "sense point of view" and can only see that which is visible, you have a problem! You can only see the face of the problem and your deficiency to handle it. If you have discovered and declared that God is the ground of all reality, then the existence of that need reminds you of something else. You look away from your own deficiencies and *see* him who is invisible through the eyes of faith. As we have already said—you look through the obvious to see the actual. Knowing that God can never allow a need to exist beyond his capacity to supply, we can then praise him for meeting that need! We do this despite the fact that there may be nothing *visible* when we begin to praise. We then, through the exercise of our belief and through an act of our will, take a trip into the realm of the unseen to bring back realities. What is reality? He who is all is reality.

"And what is faith? Faith gives substance to our hopes, and makes us certain of realities we do not see" (Heb. 11:1, NEB).

The King James Version simply states, "Now *faith is* the *substance* of things hoped for, and the *evidence* of things not seen." Get used to your new *substance* and *evidence*. THIS IS reality! Our faith "substantizes" the invisible.

WHY AM I HERE?

The purpose of a person or thing has everything to do with its existence. It is fundamental and foundational to the discovery of all the mysteries of life for us to answer the reason for our being here. Bound up in this question is the reason for our creation, as well as our salvation. It will affect every realm of our thinking and will be pivotal in developing a workable plan of economy.

God has a plan! That plan has not changed down through the centuries. He is pursuing that plan with unswerving determination. He purposes to use us to complete his plan. Listen to this!

Having made known to us the mystery of his will, according
to his good pleasure which he hath purposed in himself:
that in the dispensation of the fulness of times he might
gather together in one all things in Christ, both which are
in heaven, and which are on earth; even in him (Eph. 1:9-10).

God is up to something! He has never given up. He still pursues.
I am here on purpose. That purpose is eternal. Around that
purpose revolves the glorious truths of salvation and service. Once
this is settled, many of the heartaches that accrue to suffering
humanity will be dissolved.

Let us go back to the creation of man. God clearly disclosed
his reasons for making man when he declared, "Let us make
man in our image, after our likeness: and let them have dominion"
(Gen. 1:26). God had created a world according to divine dimensions and directions. All that exists is for the glory of God and
is a result of divine declarations. The psalmist said, "He spake,
and it was done; he commanded, and it stood fast" (Ps. 33:9).

Let us examine the statement of intention in Genesis 1:26.
God said, "Let us make man in our image." We shall never
know this side of eternity the full meaning of these words. We
can, however, draw some rather safe and rewarding conclusions.
God made man to look like himself. There is something godlike
in man and something manlike in God. They favor. This was
the divine intention. Thus, God proposed to make man an extension of his life. Now, do not allow this statement to say more
than it says, but let it say all that it says! You and I are not
God, but in our redeemed state we are God's means of extending
himself to wherever we are. Isn't that exciting? *I am here to
extend the life of God!* That is the reason for my creation, and
that is the reason for my salvation. I think that this is what Paul
had in mind when he said, "For to me to live is Christ" (Phil.
1:21). Externally, there should be that about you and me that
reminds everyone around us of God.

"After our likeness" seems to have decided *internal* implications. "In our image" suggests external likeness. In *countenance* and *conduct* man is to reflect what God is like. Someone has well said that man is essentially worth no more than what his life shows the world about God's character. We are created after the likeness of the eternal God. This has both moral and motivational implications. In our morals and motives we are to reflect God's character. Thus, I am to be not only an extension of his life . . . I am an expression of his character. If my salvation is working, my life is a fitting expression of what God is like. WOW! But how? Stay with me, and we shall view this later.

"Let them have dominion" reveals the third reason for our being here. Dominion or authority was given to man from God. It was a gift. Man did not have to work for it. It was his by divine purpose and decree. "Let them have dominion" was not just a suggestion, but an eternal decree. And man was given dominion over everything in creation. That dominion was absolute. So, man was made to be an exhibit of God's dominion and power. He ruled with authority! As long as he was in submission to authority, he possessed authority.

Thus, for all to see, here was man in the beginning:

an extension of the presence of God,
an expression of the person of God,
an exhibit of the power of God!

And who was around to see? God and the angels saw. "And God saw every thing that he had made, and, behold, it was very good" (Gen. 1:31). But alas, the devil saw it, too, and didn't like it one bit. Every time the enemy saw man, he was reminded of the *presence,* the *person,* and the *power* of God. He couldn't stand the sight of it. He went right to work planting doubts, promoting denial, prompting distrust in God's purposes. Eve sinned and gave Adam no rest until he had followed suit. The result was the fall, an event with more serious implications than the average pew-warmer realizes. Man was lost! He was lost to God's *presence,* lost to God's *person,* and lost to God's *power.* Man became, in his fallen state, an extension, not of God's presence, but of his own self-dominated presence. He became an expression, not of God's person, but of his own weak and wretched ego—a pattern of the enemy's. He became an exhibit, not of God's power, but of his own innate weakness. He lost manifestations of the family likeness. He lost the moral similitude that came with his creation. He lost the power to reign over all the earth. The devil won that round by default and by forfeit.

But God's plan is still in motion. The plan had not failed! Man had failed! In failing he became more like the one he followed (the devil) than the one in whose image he was created.

The plan need not change. It is perfect! But fallen man must be changed to be restored to the plan.

Enter the Lord Jesus Christ—the wisdom of God and the power of God! He is the answer. Jesus lived amid this earthly scene for thirty-three years, long enough to prove that a man indwelt of God could be all that a man should be.

He was the extension of the presence of God. "He that hath seen me hath seen the Father" (John 14:9).

He was the expression of the person of God. "I and my Father are one" (John 10:30).

He was the exhibit of the power of God. "All power is given unto me in heaven and in earth" (Matt. 28:18).

Jesus lived to *prove* God's *presence, person,* and *power.* He died to *purchase* us to God's *presence, person,* and *power.* NOW HE LIVES TO PROCURE IN US THE PRESENCE, PERSON, AND POWER OF GOD! Glorious salvation! I am restored to be all that God made Adam to be in the first place.

Because of the first Adam, I was born in sin—death reigned. Through the Second Adam I am restored to creation's capabilities. The first Adam in me goes to the cross and the Second Adam comes to the throne.

> I am crucified with Jesus
> And the cross has set me free

I have risen again with Jesus
And He lives and reigns in me.

Mystery his from ancient ages
But at length to faith made plain
Christ in me the hope of glory
Tell it over and over again.

THIS IS SALVATION! Jesus lives in me, having restored me
to my true humanity so that God in the totality of himself may
dwell in that humanity to *extend his presence, express his person,
and exhibit his power.*

This is the crux of salvation. This is why we are here! Any
sound plan of economy must have the issue of purpose settled.
This means that I have no reason or right to live unto myself.
I was not created for myself, but for himself and his ends. I
am here for him and him alone! I yield to that high and holy
purpose, and I yield to his glorious arrangement that declares,
"To whom God would make known what is the riches of the
glory of this mystery among the Gentiles; which is

Christ in you, the hope of glory" (Col. 1:27).

WHAT IS GOD UP TO?

This question must be answered not only in general terms with
regard to God's overall plan but also in specific terms as relating
to you and me personally. The ability to see through the eyes
of faith into that spirit dimension and behold what God is up
to in his behalf in us is an "indispensable" in living victoriously.
The terms of many a perplexing situation will be clear when
we get this vision.

What is God up to? He is building a "forever family." He
is preparing us for permanent residence in that eternal dimension.
Everything that happens here is helping prepare us. Now Jesus
lives in us to conform us into his image. On the way to glory
we are to exist to the praise of his glory (Eph. 1:12).

It is the purpose of God that on the way to glory our lives should be the laboratories in which can be demonstrated the power of the indwelling Spirit to shape men into the image of God. As that process continues, he proposes that we become redemptive in our influence on others through the indwelling Redeemer.

God is disclosing himself to the world through us. He is not hiding. As he was in Christ revealing himself to the world, Christ is in us showing the world what God is like. He is residing, ruling, and releasing his life through us to the same proportion that we are living yielded to him.

God has purchased us through the blood of Jesus and empowered us through the indwelling Spirit, that we might be involved in his eternal purposes. God is up to something. Revival is simply "getting in on what God is up to." I repeat, man must get off of what he is down to and in on what God is up to. If he doesn't, he is going to wind up out of it!

God is in the process of gathering together in one all things in Christ. The word used in Ephesians 1:10 is *dispensation*. While we often use that term to denote a specific season or period of time, the literal rendering is "the management of a household." The word is *oikonomia* taken from two Greek words, *oikos* for *house* and *nomos* for *rule*. Our word *economy* is an obvious derivative from the Greek term and fittingly so.

Paul states in Colossians 1:25 that he was "made a minister according to the dispensation of God." In other words, God did what he did on the basis of rules and plans which he himself drew up. He is not making up the plan as he goes along, but is executing an eternal plan according to exact details.

God instigated his plan on this earth at the dawn of creation and has pursued it with dauntless determination. He will not be deterred. His plan involves everybody and everything. Nothing exists without purpose. Nobody lives bereft of purpose! THERE IS A PLAN—a plan you and I can get in on. It is God's plan! That plan will still be being carried out 100,000,000 years from this very moment! Choose his plan!

In brief fashion we have sought to answer three great, grave questions. WHAT IS REALITY? God is the source of all reality. WHY AM I HERE? We are here as manifestations of that reality. WHAT IS GOD UP TO? He is executing his eternal plan to glorify himself and desires to include every one of us in that plan.

NOW, ON TO THE MAIN BUSINESS!

The main business of man is God and his business! It seems that in these days of religious excitement, when we have had some indications of a moving in the tops of the mulberries, that many of us have missed the point. We are not saved for us . . . we are saved because of him and for him. We are not to be filled with the Spirit for us, but for him. His blessings come to us, not just to make life enjoyable but to make us employable to his glory.

A "self point of view" must be exchanged for a "God point of view." We are not in the business of life for ourselves, but for him. He made us for himself, and we can have no real meaning to life until we exist wholly for him. That's what eternity is all about! That's what salvation is all about. That's what God's plan of economy is all about. That's what this volume is all about. I want you to get this clear before we go on. Through the principles disclosed in this book, your whole economy will change if you apply them . . . but this is not for you—it is for him! Blessings will come to you in every realm of your life, but I want you to understand that it is for him! You will know sufficiency and satisfaction as you have never known it before—but it is not for you—it is for him!

It is *in* him that we live and move and have our being. It is *unto* him that we should be to the praise of his glory. It is *through* him that we are enabled to be what he redeemed us to be.

Now on to the main business . . . HIS!

2
THE PLATFORM OF THE PLAN

"Any plan of economy is constructed on a platform of principles. These may be right or wrong, but the plan will be as strong as the rightness or as weak as the wrongness of those principles."

In this chapter I propose to build a platform upon which the plan of God can be put on exhibit. There are many ways of saying what I am going to say in this division. This is simply the manner in which God has lead me to declare it. These principles, in similar form, are found in a previous volume, *One Home Under God* in the chapter "Victory in Family Finances." This chapter is foundational in that the remainder of the volume will be an amplification of the principles stated herein. These principles have proved to be liberating in many lives and realms of life. I challenge you to examine them for veracity and apply them for victory. Do not go on to another until you have digested the first, and so on. You will find them, in some cases, cutting across everything you have believed in the realm of economy. This chapter may be detrimental to your present plan of economy! Remember that God's thoughts are not our thoughts, and his ways are not our ways. Seven planks in the platform follow.

PLANK NUMBER ONE: GOD POSSESSES AND PRESIDES OVER ALL THE WEALTH IN THIS WORLD AND THE NEXT.

Now this is a sweeping declaration and invites investigation. I want to examine with you the four parts of this statement. Being the first, it is absolutely basic. If we cannot agree on this fact we cannot go on.

First, God possesses all. God is still the sole owner of this universe. Man may refuse to acknowledge this and draw up his own papers denoting possession but God is still the owner. Man may garner the resources and put a price tag for sale or lease but it all belongs to God. The psalmist declared, "The earth is the Lord's, and the fulness thereof; the world, and they that dwell therein (Ps. 24:1). That fact is eternal and unchanging. We must not allow our apparent freedom to use what is his to keep us from remembering that it is still his! He didn't put a mark of his ownership on the meadow . . . but every meadow in the world is his. He didn't put a NO TRESPASSING sign on the mountains . . . but they are his! He didn't ration the fresh air and breezes which blow . . . but they are all his! He didn't put a tax on the vastness of the reaches of space . . . but they are his! When our astronauts landed on the moon, they didn't find his footprints before them but he had been there . . . the moon is his. And when we get close enough to see Mars and Jupiter, we may not see the fingerprints of God . . . but he has been there, and they are his. He doesn't draw royalty on the beautiful songs of the birds, but every bird and song belong to him. He doesn't send a notice saying RENT DUE . . . but we are camping on his property, breathing his air, spending his time! We house our spirits in bodies . . . and everything belongs to him. Our spirits are his. He is Spirit, and we are but extensions of him. We live in bodies which exist according to God-ordained principles. We could not live a second without them or apart from them. We are his!

God possesses it all,—certainly, but doesn't the devil have a lot of it? Yes, the devil seems to have a lot of it in his custody, but only with God's permission! God still owns it!

David, in that majestic hour when the great offering was taken for the building of the Temple which amounted to the equivalent of billions of today's dollars, attested to God's universal ownership. In his unforgettable offering doxology he said, "Thine, O

Lord, is the greatness, and the power, and the glory, and the victory, and the majesty: for all that is in the heaven and in the earth is thine; thine is the kingdom, O Lord, and thou art exalted as head above all" (1 Chron. 29:11).

Since we have already asserted that all reality is bound up in him, we should have no difficulty in believing that he is sole possessor of the sum total of all manifestations of reality . . . temporal and eternal. Romans 11:36 is again appropriate: "For of him, and through him, and to him, are all things."

> My Father is rich in houses and lands,
> He holdeth the wealth of the world in His hands!
> Of rubies and diamonds, of silver and gold,
> His coffers are full, He has riches untold.

Second, God presides over all that is his. Now this gave me some problems at first. The devil and the devil's crowd seem to have so much of this world's wealth tied up. This struck me as I drove down the Las Vegas strip several years ago. Signs on either side of the street inviting patronage lighted the midnight sky like noonday. Some of those signs cost more than a million dollars! If God presides over all his wealth, why does the devil have so much? I am not sure I have all the answers to my own question. But I am sure of this—that God could call for all that is his at any time and put man out of business. He has the powers of the universe at his disposal and could collect it all in a matter of moments. Did not the enemy rest on the riches of Caanan until God's people got there? Somebody had to take care of it during those interim years while it waited for the coming of the people of God. My Father *owns* it all and is *over* it all. That gives me so much joy! My Father owns Nelson Rockefeller, J. Paul Getty, and the Onassis millions! Don't sell God short! He has resources that have never been tapped!

David further declared in that doxology in 1 Chronicles 29:12, "Both riches and honour come of thee, and thou reignest over all; and in thine hand is power and might; and in thine hand it is to make great, and to give strength unto all." The One who has all power has all wealth! It is his when he wants to come calling for it.

Jesus declared, "All power is given unto me in heaven and in earth" (Matt. 28:18). That simply means that HE IS IN CONTROL! Look out, world, you belong to my Father!

Third, "all the wealth" simply refers to everything, every commodity everywhere. We tend to give things a measure of value commensurate with the demand and supply ratio. Diamonds are very expensive. Gold is going up! Real estate is out of sight. Air is free, even though it is becoming increasingly polluted. Time is of great value! Love is priceless. Fellowship has no price tag, but of what worth it is! Lump it all together—the seen, the unseen, the tangible, the intangible, dollars, drachmas, marks, yen, power, love, peace of heart—everything is His! His is the greatness, and the power, and the glory, and the majesty, and the victory! David said as he blessed the Lord in the midst of the congregation, "For all things come of thee" (1 Chron. 29:14).

Fourth, "In this world and the next" denotes universality in time, space, and dimension. David's inclusion of "everything in heaven and earth" not only meant everything in the now everywhere, but everything for all time. He presides over two realms: time and eternity; seen and unseen. Who knows what lies beneath the surface of this astounding earth upon which we live? Who can tell what untapped caches of enormous wealth wait for man's investigations and appropriations. Who knows but that in the very makeup of the air which we breathe and through which we walk, there are revelations of untold resources. Limitless resources boggle the mind when we begin to reason of the wealth held in the lap of the mighty oceans, or within the walls of the majestic mountain ranges, or beneath the fathoms of polar snows and ice. The undeveloped real estate across this wide world is in the billions of acres, and every square inch is filled with vast wealth. Who can tell us that God will not allow us to make discoveries which would change the polar caps into verdant valleys and fertile plains and the sprawling Saharas into tropical paradises? The wealth of this world is unfathomable! But that is just this world!

What of that other world of entities money cannot buy, entities that are available to us now, not just later on? Paul declares God "hath blessed us with all spiritual blessings in heavenly places in Christ." The heavenly places may not be heaven, but indeed *right here* existing concurrently with time and space, but available to us on another frequency. Who can put a price tag on love, or announce the true value of self-esteem, or present an accurate estimate on respect. These are some of the riches of the next world which are ours now! All this and the gift of faith which is God's arrangement for rendering that which is eternal ours in time and space, of reckoning the unseen real substance, of accounting that which is future—*now!*

Think of it: *My Father and yours possesses and presides over all the wealth in this world and the next.* Say that out loud until your heart says, "AMEN!" Our Father has it all!

PLANK NUMBER TWO: GOD WANTS HIS WEALTH IN CIRCULATION.

> A bell is not a bell until you ring it,
> A song is not a song until you sing it,
> A joy is not a joy until you share it,
> Love is not love until you give it away,
> Wealth is not wealth until you circulate it.

The nature of true wealth is such that it cannot be stored. When it is stored or hoarded, it ceases to be beneficial and, thus, ceases to be true wealth. This principle rests upon several observations.

First, there is God's nature. It is the nature of God to give. God loved the world and gave his own Son! God is a giving God, declaring that we cannot outgive him. He tells us in Malachi 3:10, "prove me now herewith, saith the Lord of hosts, if I will not open you the windows of heaven, and pour you out a blessing, that there shall not be room enough to receive it." God is ever giving!

Second, there is the life-style of Jesus. Jesus himself was God's wealth in circulation. He deliberately put himself in circulation and did not take himself out until he had been spent to purchase redemption for us. He was always giving and seldom receiving. Those who center their lives around him and truly become his disciples strangely discover this life-style becoming theirs without really having to try. It just seems natural that we should give since we are in love with Him. He gave up his glory, his equality with God, his riches in heaven. He gave his time, his love, and his consideration during the days of his life on earth. He wound up giving his life. He is still giving.

Third, there is the law of nature that demonstrates the fact that God wants his wealth in circulation. There is written within the context of nature a certain law of *mutual beneficence.* In the unfallen earth this law was in operation, and the results were glorious. There was plenty of everything, and everything alive in the earth seemed to have one theme . . . GIVE, GIVE, GIVE! The sun gave! The earth gave! The animals gave! Man gave! The trees gave! This glorious giving cycle continued until sin and death reigned. The enemy introduced a new concept into the human spirit . . . GET, GET, GET! Man became a greedy getter instead of a gracious giver! He then began to guard, get, keep, and hoard. Man's philosophy in general today is:

> Get all you can,
> Can all you get,
> Sit on the lid,
> And poison the rest!

I am convinced that there are no true shortages in the world overall . . . just a terrifying imbalance brought about and maintained by the sinfulness of man. The world has been thrown into imbalance by man's greed and selfishness. The philosophy of giving is an absolute necessity of life on earth. If we cease to give, we cease to live and vice versa. Once, I was roaming the woods in Colorado and came across some true lilies of the valley. They are very small flowers with a striking fragrance. I bent down to smell them. I do not remember a sweeter or more appealing aroma. What amazed me was that I could not "smell up" all the fragrance. I supposed it had done that ever since it had bloomed and would continue it after I left. I plucked one of them, and in a matter of minutes I noticed that the fragrance was gone! With death the giving stopped.

The case for hoarding cannot be supported by the Scriptures. I am sure that there is nothing wrong with being sensible in preparing for the seasons of need or saving wisely, but there is no way to justify needless hoarding of wealth of any kind.

Fourth, the suggestion of Scripture supports the theory of circulation. The preacher in Ecclesiastes 5:13-14 said, "There is a sore evil which I have seen under the sun, namely, riches kept for the owners thereof to their hurt. But those riches perish by evil travail: and he begetteth a son, and there is nothing in his hand."

Jesus said, "Give, and it shall be given unto you" (Luke 6:38). The proper circulation of wealth is a basic principle in a stable, working plan of economy. Any system of economy breaks down when vast amounts of resources are hoarded and taken out of circulation. *I am convinced that God will entrust to us as much as we can be trusted to be put into circulation for his glory and the reaching of souls.*

God wants his wealth in circulation. He is dependent upon you and me to help him get it into circulation. This is exciting! God wants me to help give away his wealth, all kinds of wealth! There is plenty!

PLANK NUMBER THREE: ALL OF GOD'S WEALTH LE-
GALLY BELONGS TO HIS CHILDREN.

God has no wealth that does not belong to his children. You
cannot simply say, "It is his!" You can just as rightly say, "It
is mine!" We are Abraham's seed and heirs according to the
promise. The blessings of Abraham are ours.

Paul reminds us that we have been blessed with all spiritual
blessings in the heavenly places in Christ Jesus. (Eph. 1:3)

He reminds us again in Romans 8:32 that we have been given
all things through Christ.

He said to young Timothy, "Trust . . . in the living God, who
giveth us richly all things to enjoy" (1 Tim. 6:17).

Peter calls on us to remember that we have been given according to his divine power all things that pertain to life and godliness
(2 Pet. 1:3).

We are told in 1 Corinthians 3:21-23: "Therefore let no man
glory in men. For all things are yours; whether Paul, or Apollos,
or Cephas, or the world, or life, or death, or things present,
or things to come; all are yours; and ye are Christ's; and Christ
is God's."

We have been informed that we are joint-heirs with Christ
(Rom. 8:17). We are not equal heirs but joint-heirs. We have
it all with him! The testator has died and has bequeathed all
the wealth to us. The will has been probated and the testator
resurrected and appointed as administrator to appropriate by
his life all that he purchased by his death. He lives in us by
his Spirit to make real and realize everything he redeemed us
to have and to be! Through this means all of God's wealth is
ours.

We are called in 1 Corinthians 4, "stewards." We saw that
oikonomia meant *house rule.* The word for steward is *oikonomos*
or *one who manages or rules a house.* A steward is one who
manages another's property. It is the choice of a steward to be
a good steward or a bad steward. A good steward is one who
recognizes the value of what he possesses and wisely manages

it to the glory of the one who owns it. A poor steward is one
who does not recognize the value of what he has, or who does
not wisely put what he has to use.

God has entrusted the wealth that belongs to him in every
realm into our hands and expects an accounting. It is both good
and bad that this wealth belongs to us. It is good if we acknowledge our stewardship, appropriate those riches, and apply the
rules of His Lordship. It is bad if we live as paupers with all
this wealth, or misuse it on ourselves.

Can you believe it? Can you really believe that all God's
wealth, all the wealth in every realm, seen and unseen, belongs
to us?

The obvious question follows hard upon this revelation: if I
am an heir, where are my riches? If it is all mine, then where
is it and why can't I appropriate it? We will allow the next
plank to answer that question for us.

PLANK NUMBER FOUR: THE WAY TO APPROPRIATE GOD'S WEALTH IS TO GIVE.

Now this makes little sense to the human senses. Little of what
God says makes sense to our senses. That which may be known
in the spirit realm is not conceivable to the senses.

This is one of the most astounding spiritual principles in the
entire Bible. The results of applying this principle are miraculous!
It will work in every realm. The principle is so vital to our
getting in on God's plan of economy that I am going to spend
an entire chapter amplifying it.

God created within the context of the whole universe a giving
disposition. There is built into the floor of his creation a law
of mutual beneficence. Living things give and receive, and in
this blessed cycle there is the perpetuation of life. God made
man to give. When man changed his basic philosophy from the
giving reference to the getting reference, he suffered death to
that part of him which responded to God. That death becomes
life only when we give our hearts to Jesus and give him a place

of lordship in our lives. We then move back into the giving cycle
again and set the amount of wealth by the amount of our giving.
Jesus said, "Give, and it shall be given unto you; good measure,
pressed down, and shaken together, and running over, shall men
give unto your bosom. *For with the same measure that ye mete
withal it shall be measured to you again*" (Luke 6:38).

That one verse, when believed and applied, will be the means
of a miracle in every area of your life in which you are determined
to apply the principle. This is such a vital principle that we
shall cover it more fully under the chapter entitled "The Plan
in a Word" which follows in this volume.

PLANK NUMBER FIVE: WE ARE TO GIVE, NOT ACCORDING TO OUR APPARENT WEALTH, BUT ACCORDING TO GOD'S ACTUAL WEALTH.

It is here that we encounter two kinds of giving: *reason* giving
and *revelation* giving. Most folks give whatever they give according to what they can afford. These cannot be happy givers because
when you give as much as you can afford you have given until
it hurts. A *hurting* giver is not a *happy* giver. He has given until
he can afford to give no more according to his own estimation.
We have many people who give until it hurts, and they simply
continue to hurt. When they part with that which they give,
their countenance seems to say of their gifts: "When we asunder
part, it gives us inward pain!"

Reason giving depends upon human calculation for determining the amount to be given. Love, time, concern, and money
are meted out according to human figuring. One surveys his own
account of his account. He says, "Now, let's see . . . I have
so much and, thus, I believe that I can afford to give this much."
God is not consulted. Only the human reason determines how
and how much was given. This is virtually the universal method
of giving to religious causes today, and it has gone unchallenged.
It is bringing in some gifts but is not bringing the joy intended
for the cheerful giver.

Revelation giving is that which depends upon a divine revelation for the amount to be given. Revelation giving takes into account what is in His account upon which we can draw.

I shall never forget when we first began to learn as a family and as a church how to get in on revelation giving. Our church faced the challenge of building and raising the entire amount needed among the membership. As we came to the conviction that God's people could care for any needs that God had brought about through his power, we set our faces to raise a large sum of money. We knew that it would take the power of God to motivate and enable his people to get this done. I faced the challenge for myself and presented it to my people. We asked the Lord how much and how we were to give. Have you ever begun to "how about" God? That is what I began to do to arrive at *my figure* for what He would *have me give!* I said, "God, *how about* $1,000?" There was no answer from God and no satisfaction for my heart. I said, "God, *how about* $2,000?" Still no word from God and no satisfaction for my seeking heart. I was already far past my sense of what I could afford. I didn't even know where I would have gotten $1,000! Finally, I said in sheer desperation, "All right, Lord, how much?" A figure came to me five times the original amount. I tried to blame it on the devil or on my imagination, but I could not get away from it. This was what the Taylors committed themselves for and you know the story! *God enabled us to do what he revealed that we should do!* In fact, we were able to go above and beyond to the glory of God! Praise the Lord! For once we had given according to revelation and not according to reason! The overall results throughout the membership were astounding. Folks walked into a financial miracle when they started giving according to God's account, and not according to their account.

Whose resources have you been taking into account as you have determined the amount and program of your giving? If it has been calculated according to your apparent resources, your program has been dull, unchallenging, and unrewarding in comparison to what it can be. I believe that this principle alone would revolutionize the life of any church or institution if its constituents would begin to employ *revelation* giving. Revelation giving is built on the following reasoning:

God knows what the need is.

God knows how much he wants to make available through me.

God is pleased to let me know what he wants to give through me.

God will enable me to be sufficient to do anything which he leads me to give.

When I give from his resources instead of mine, I do not have to be limited by the amount of my resources.

This is giving which requires the presence and power of God.

This is giving which glorifies God and grows up the believer.

Now, let me remind you that I am talking about all kinds of giving . . . not merely money. True stewardship involves all the commodities of life.

I am convinced that revelation giving is a kind of giving that all too few people know anything about. We have not trained them in principles of spiritual giving and, thus, have kept them from the supreme joy of godly giving.

PLANK NUMBER SIX: IT IS PROFITABLE TO GIVE GOD'S WAY.

Nowhere is there the command to give without a promise of return on the investment. Yet, there are those who say that we are never to give with a view of profit! I say to this . . . *It is according to whose profit you seek!* Since every command to give is followed by a promise to receive, then I am to give expectant of a return. It is what I do with that return that is important! I am to give to get to give to get to give! And it should always end in increased giving!

In a former principle we looked at the startling words of Jesus, "Give, and it shall be given unto you." Here is a command and a promise. If we were not to have a return in view, then why should Jesus mention it?

Do you remember what Paul said in 2 Corinthians 9:6? "He which soweth sparingly shall also reap sparingly; and he which soweth bountifully shall reap also bountifully." Thus, you have the principle: sparing sowing—sparing reaping; bountiful sowing—bountiful reaping. There is the simple promise that the more you sow, the more you will reap.

The writer of Proverbs reminds us, "Honour the Lord with thy substance, and with the first fruits of thine increase: so shall thy barns be filled with plenty, and thy presses shall burst out with new wine" (Prov. 3:9-10). This again is a simple promise that he who gives will receive in return.

The promise that the righteous will flourish and prosper is to be seen many times in the Scriptures. This promise has not been withdrawn! Proverbs 11:28 says, "He that trusteth in his riches shall fall: but the righteous shall flourish as a branch."

God promised in Malachi 3:10 that if the people were faithful in tithes and offerings he would pour them out a blessing they would not have room enough to receive. Furthermore, he promised to rebuke the devourer of their crops for their sakes (Mal. 3:11). Friend, that is a good deal in anybody's estimation. You be faithful to obey God's command, and God will be faithful to look after your interests.

Peter one day must have felt in a pious mood. (I guess we all have those days!) He said to Jesus, "Lo, we have left all, and followed thee" (Mark 10:28). He must have expected to receive commendation for all that he had left behind to take up with Jesus. After all, he had left a great deal! He had left dirty, broken nets and stinking fish and a motley mob of friends! Whatever answer he expected from Jesus, he received the unexpected. Of that I am sure! Jesus said, "Verily, I say unto you, There is no man that hath left house, or brethren, or sisters, or father, or mother, or wife, or children, or lands, for my sake and the gospel's, but he shall receive an hundredfold now in this time, houses, and brethren, and sisters, and mothers, and children, and lands, with persecutions; and in the world to come eternal life" (Mark 10:29-30). A hundred to one return on your investment!

If I were to make a public announcement of the opening of an investment program with that kind of return, I would be in danger of getting trampled under the response! Yet, this is exactly what Jesus promises. You may be thinking, "Well, I know that it will prove a good investment in eternity to invest in the things of the Lord!" Friend, we do not need to wait for eternity! Notice the words in that passage "now in this time." Have you had to give up something because you followed the Lord? He will make it up to you with profit! That is a promise!

Now, stop being apologetic about expecting a return on your investment in the things of God. He wants to get you in on his giving program, and when he can trust you, he will fill your coffers full, so you may "abound unto every good work."

Before I leave this point, let me mention something that I only recently discovered. There are several kinds of giving. One of these is giving to the poor. I read in the Bible these words, "He that hath pity upon the poor lendeth unto the Lord; and that which he hath given will he pay him again" (Prov. 19:17). Now, isn't that some kind of giving? I could hardly believe it. Jesus called this alms giving. I thought when I read this passage, "I wouldn't mind giving the Lord a loan. I believe that he can be trusted to pay it back!" I quickly told my church about this Scriptural discovery, and we immediately took up an offering for the poor! We simply gave it to the poor. They are never hard to find. Immediately reports began to come in from people who were finding that God hastened his word to perform it. I have never since been guilty of begrudging the gifts to the poor. Giving to the poor is just another way to release the riches of God upon our circumstances. Hallelujah!

PLANK NUMBER SEVEN: GOD LOVES A HILARIOUS GIVER.

"Every man according as he purposeth in his heart, so let him give; not grudgingly, or of necessity: for God loveth a cheerful giver" (2 Cor. 9:7). Did you know that the Greek word for *cheerful* is literally the word for *hilarious*. In fact our word *hilarious* is a transliteration of the Greek word *hilaros*.

While it is true that God has no favorites according to worthiness (for we are all unworthy), he does have a special place in his heart for a hilarious giver! I believe that all heaven gets excited when someone discovers the secrets of hilarious giving!

Can you imagine the angels in heaven talking? One says to another, "You know, this fellow I am assigned to just won't believe God for anything! He is greedy and has no idea what is waiting for him if he will just give! I wish I could get a transfer!" Another chimes in to say, "I have never been so happy! This fellow that I am assigned to has just discovered that he cannot outgive God, and he has gone absolutely wild giving here and giving there! Praise the Lord!" If God loves a cheerful giver, then the angels must love the cheerful giver as well! What must your angel be saying about your giving?

Are you a cheerful, hilarious giver? There is a way to be one! I am going to deal with this more extensively in a subsequent chapter entitled "Becoming a Hilarious Giver."

Now again and again in this chapter I have mentioned the medium of money as one of the things we can give. This, however, does not cover a fraction of it! The rules of giving cover all the commodities that can be given. We have much to give. We have time, talents, love, concern, respect, joy, esteem, thoughtfulness, physical commodities which can benefit others, and money!

When it comes to the giving of money, the question arises about the tithe. This is not a volume about the tithe, for obvious reasons. There are many volumes written about the tithe. I am convinced that we have emphasized the tithe at the expense of an emphasis on Spirit-directed giving. When one begins to tithe, he has stopped robbing God. He has begun to give God only what is *due him under the law*. That is all! The tithe is a good place to start, but a terrible place to stop in giving. Beyond the tithe there is the offering. There is absolutely no limit on how much this may be. This is where we begin to practice the principles of godly giving. This is where the hilarious part comes in. We have discussed the matter of giving to the poor. This can hardly be categorized as an offering, since it is considered a loan to the Lord, and the Lord pays off such loans with interest! Praise the Lord!

Now before you leave this chapter, I want you to go back over these seven planks in the platform of God's miraculous economy. I want you to investigate them and seek to protest them. I want you to try them in the light of the Scriptures you know or can find. I want you at this point either to disbelieve and drop the whole matter (and give the book to someone who will believe), or to believe and get ready for the adventure of your life . . . GETTING IN ON GOD'S MIRACULOUS PLAN OF ECONOMY!

Ready? Let's go!

3
THE PLAN IN OPERATION

The Christian lives in two worlds at the same time. The sense world is seeking to bring us into bondage to its rules and its life-style. It is always pulling us down to earth like the power of gravity. It is relentless. I was born into this sense world a good many years ago when I was born physically. Sometime later I was born into the spirit world when I received Jesus Christ as my Savior and was born again. I found out that when I was born again, I was born into a world of reality which could be more real than the reality of the sense world. I discovered that I did not have to allow the world of the senses to squeeze me into its mold.

The sense world is always applying its pressures to conform. The sense world denies and disregards the truths of the Scriptures that are eternal and unchanging. The sense world would keep us from enjoying the riches of that other unseen world into which dimension we were born when we were born the second time.

Contrary to popular opinion, the supply of the believer is not this world. Too many believers have made this world the total source of their supply. Thus, they are poor and too often have to sing . . .

> "Here I wander like a beggar
> Through the heat and through the cold."

We need to discover the source of our supply! Jesus Christ is in us. He is the same in us as he is in heaven. He has brought into our lives the total wealth of heaven. Thus, the total wealth of heaven is in us! Paul affirms that we have been blessed with all spiritual blessings in heavenly places in Christ Jesus. That is the key! All our wealth is in Jesus! In him is the untold and untapped supply for all of our needs and all of our desires. We are living in the realms and reaches of the wealth of Jesus. Why aren't we enjoying it? Because we have allowed the economy of this world to set our rules, to draw the lines of our activity, and to be the source of our supply. We have lost in the midst of the rules of this earth the real, eternal plan of economy that will stand when the stars begin to fall.

Listen, *I for one do not want to be bound to the rules of the economy of this world when there is a plan as infinitely superior to it as eternity is superior to time!* I want in on that plan. How about you?

In this chapter we will see that plan in operation in a familiar story in the Old Testament. The narrative is found in 2 Kings 4:1-7.

This is a fantastic story of a woman who found the true source of her supply. You will remember that Elisha ministered in a day when the sons of the prophets were in the land. One of them had died and left a widow and two young sons. The creditor had demanded payment on unpaid debts and threatened to take the two young sons as slaves if prompt payment was not made. It was at this point that the prophet Elisha came into the picture. She cried to Elisha regarding her need. We shall divide the story into four movements: The Demand, The Desperation, The Dependence, and The Deliverance.

THE DEMAND
The plan of God is often thrown into gear in a great need, a great demand. Sometimes in the midst of that great demand, we discover that the former source of our supply can no longer

be depended on. This woman had looked to her husband as the source of her supply for years. There had been no cause to trust God on her part during that time. The supply was presumed to be taken care of by her husband. But alas, the source of her supply was suddenly removed. How often God allows this to happen so that we will find out where we should look for our supply.

Her husband was suddenly taken, and there was left a great indebtedness and no means of revenue. She was in a situation in which she was thrown upon the only source available, the resources of God! If God did not come through for her, she could not live. God had engineered her circumstances to move her into a position to trust him as her only supply. God had allowed her to get in need in order that he could be her supply! God had *allowed* her need in order to *meet* her need. What providence! He planned to get that woman in on his riches and would not spare the circumstances to bring her in! My friend, that is love! Praise the Lord! God, if you will have it, will do the same for you.

There is a law operating in the spiritual realm that necessitates problems, needs, demands. God only supplies when there is need. Why should he supply when there is no need. Even in the realm of the natural, the supply meets the need. In the law of aerodynamics, the need brings about the supply. As the airplane speeds down the runway the friction and antagonism of the wings moving through the air raise the giant missile into the air. Need is created, and the need is supplied by the law. The airplane is making a demand, and the law is providing the needs. This woman had to be put into a situation in such deep need that God had to overcome her self-sufficiency in order to become her sufficiency himself!

Whatever is really needed is supplied. Most of us are not really out where we have chosen to put ourselves in such need that God must come through with heaven's resources.

A friend of mine recently was approached by a lad who stated a desire to have the power of God upon his life. My friend asked him what he was now doing that made a demand on the power of God. The lad was made to see that he was engaged in nothing that was making a demand on the resources of God's power. He was doing everything that he was doing, and no need called for God's power. He wasn't using the power that was available to him. The woman in 2 Kings found herself in a situation which demanded that she draw from the resources of God.

The demand brought her to the prophet of God. Why did she come to him? The simple answer is that his life-style was one which depended on God. He was of that school which believed that the very existence of a need was the guarantee of its supply. For God could not allow a need to exist beyond his power to supply. *Elisha* had followed in the steps of *Elijah* who had learned that God was the total source of his supply (Cf. 1 Kings 17:1-16). Elijah had retreated during a drought to the brook where ravens brought him meat and bread every day. When the brook went dry, he was ordered to go to Zarephath. There in miraculous circumstances God proved himself to be the ample supply to his needs and to all others who would apply the principles of eternal economy. The widow of Zarephath responded to the needs of the man of God and got in on God's plan of economy. The meal had run out, as had the oil, but when an investment was made in the kingdom by faith, that cruse of oil and that barrel of meal did not fail! Elisha had learned from Elijah where his supply was!

Friend, are you in need? If you are, praise the Lord! Only a need will bring you into contact with the true supply. God has stated in his Word his ability and willingness to meet your need. See in your situation of need not reasons for *panic* but reasons for *praise*. Panic only adds to the frustration of continued desperation, while praise points to the source of the supply.

THE DESPERATION

That widow of 2 Kings 4 was absolutely desperate! Folks

usually are when they come to the preacher. He is usually the last resort.

Look at her situation! Her source of revenue was completely cut off. Her creditor was making demands that she could not possibly meet. Her two sons were about to be taken from her as slaves of the creditor. Now that is what I call a desperate situation! Her desperation drove her to the man of God. Let us see the results of her desperation.

First, her desperation removed all trust in former sources of revenue. As long as she had something she could trust in, she would not trust the program of God. It is the same with us. As long as we have a means or a hope, we will not turn in desperation to trust the Lord. As long as her husband lived, she trusted him as the source of all her need. Now desperation saw her without anyone to trust in but the Lord. And before you say, "How terrible!" I want to ask you, "Is it so terrible that we are brought to the place where we have no one in whom to trust but the Lord?" God engineers such circumstances to throw us upon his providence.

Second, her desperation brought her to investigate the secrets of the man of God. You see, in times of desperation, it all depends upon your point of view. When this widow thought of her situation, all she could think of was a *dead husband, an empty vessel, and a crowding creditor.* That was all the point of reference she had. She had not built up a memory bank of situations in which God had met her needs. When the man of God saw need and the end of human resources, he saw ravens, a barrel of meal which did not run out, and a cruse of oil whose supply did not cease. When he saw need, he saw the mighty hand of God. When she saw need, she saw panic. That is the difference in panic and praise. It's all in the point of view.

> "Two men looked out of prison bars,
> The one saw mud and the other stars."

Third, her desperation brought an admission of total deficiency and dependence. She said, "Thine handmaid hath not any thing in the house, save a pot of oil" (2 Kings 4:2). There is something liberating about the admission, "I can't!" It somehow throws us into another dimension. Until we come to that frank admission, we are hung up at dead center. There is nothing wrong with desperation if that desperation drives us to dependence upon God. In fact, you will find that God's miracles were performed upon the platform of man's desperation. Praise the Lord for desperation!

Fourth, her desperation moved her to an act of blind, obedient faith. The man of God ordered her to go borrow vessels from the neighbors and added the words, "Not a few!" She should have taken careful note of these key words, for she was to set the amount of her own wealth by the number of vessels she brought back. She surely did not understand that command, but desperation leads one to do strange things. A desperate person usually does not quibble over details. In the back of her mind it must have sounded silly to go borrow vessels when there was nothing visible to put in them . . . but go she did! And it was further folly in her mind when the man of God told her to shut herself in and pour from the original vessel of oil and set aside that which was full. But her total desperation led to obedient faith. She did as she was told! Certainly it did not make sense. The spirit world never makes sense to the sense world.

THE DEPENDENCE

First, there is the dependence of the man of God upon his God. If we are not careful we shall overlook the key fact in the story as far as getting need and supply together . . . namely the ability of the man of God to see the *source.* He saw the situation as clearly as the widow, but he also saw something else. He saw a God who was and is in the oil business. He looked into that other world where the supplies to our need are stored. The need simply reminded him that heaven had plenty of oil.

Isn't it interesting that God started at the point of what little she had. Here again is the principle of giving. How did she know that what she was pouring out wouldn't go back to the neighbors? When she poured what she had, the miracle occurred. God's economy was thrown into gear. The man of God stood back and watched as the needs of earth and the resources of heaven got together! He was a man whose life-style was one of total dependence on God.

Second, there is the dependence of the woman on the dependence of the man of God. How often God uses someone else's faith to stir up our own. God sometimes waits for our faith, and allows our faith to be nurtured by the faith of another. The woman's record of dependence on God was weak, so she depended on Elisha's dependence. Hers was an act of faith helped by Elisha's faith. Thus, we are help to each other.

Look at the *power* of deliverance. When that blessed woman obeyed the man of God in an act of faith, God's power was released, and a different set of rules began to be applied. The woman entered a new dimension of life! God's power was set in motion by her simple act of obedient faith. So it will be with us. A *demand* we cannot *supply* leads to a *desperation* we cannot *solve* which leads to a *dependence we* cannot *substitute* which leads to a *deliverance* we cannot *stop*. The power of God was manifested just at the time of obedience.

Look, next, at the *program* of deliverance. Not only was the fact of her faith primary in bringing her deliverance, but also the amount of her faith was vital to the magnitude of her deliverance. She was asked to go borrow vessels from her neighbors. The man of God said, "Borrow not a few!" When she shut herself in, she closed the door on the number of vessels she had borrowed and, thus, the amount of oil that God could supply. God could supply no more oil than the total capacity of the vessels which she had borrowed. She had set the amount of her miracle. Isn't that a sobering thought? We set the amount of our wealth by our expectant and obedient faith.

Do you remember what Mary, the mother of Jesus, said when she was informed by heaven that she was to be so favored among women? She said, "Be it unto me according to thy word" (Luke 1:38). The widow was given no limit on how many vessels she could bring in. God had enough oil to fill every vessel in town, had she brought them. Are you ready to say to the Lord, "Be it unto me according to thy word!"? You, not God, will set the magnitude of your miracle. The program of that widow's provision and deliverance was regulated by her faith. She asked her son to bring yet another vessel and he said, "There is not a vessel more." The Bible then says, "And the oil stayed" (2 Kings 4:6). That is, the flow stopped. The flow need not have stopped. The only reason it stopped was that there was no vessel in which to pour more oil. The power of God waits for its *manifestation* and *magnitude* upon the *fact* and *fullness* of our *faith*. Little faith, little manifestation and magnitude . . . much faith, mighty manifestation and magnitude!

Look, next, at the *purpose* of deliverance. The prophet simply said, "Go, sell the oil and pay thy debt, and live thou and thy children on the rest." The need was met, the debt was paid, the sons redeemed, their livelihood was secure, and God was glorified. God is always glorified when the needs of his children are met. Look, finally, at the *person* of the deliverer. We learn much about God from a story like this, and this in part is the purpose of deliverance . . . that we might see the Deliverer. We see him as the Engineer of our circumstances who brings us into such conflict and deficiency that we are willing to thrust ourselves upon him, so he might manifest himself as our Deliverer. Elisha could well represent our Savior, the Lord Jesus, who brings our deliverance and points to our Deliverer.

God is looking for folks to stand between heaven and earth to distribute heaven's wealth everywhere! In the process, the needs of the distributor will be amply met. A verse that we shall deal with later on reminds us of this. "And God is able to make all grace abound toward you; *that ye, always having*

all sufficiency in all things, may abound to every good work"
(2 Cor. 9:8). The sufficiency in all things pertaining to us is
necessary before the needs of others can be met through us.

Right at this very moment, do you know what God is doing?
I believe that he is doing what he was doing when it was recorded
in 2 Chronicles 16:9: "For the eyes of the Lord run to and fro
throughout the whole earth, to shew himself strong in the behalf
of them whose heart is perfect toward him." Let me ask you
if you have given God cause to look at you and choose you as
one through whom to manifest his mighty power. God is not
looking for mighty men but for simple folks with hearts right
toward him. This is always his *platform* for *performance.*

The hope of our world lies in the fact God is able! His ability
can only be thrown into motion when we come to the end of
our hoarded resources and put ourselves out upon him. When
people, institutions, and churches cease to function in the power
of human energy and plug into the unlimited resources of that
other world, we will have supernatural entities manifesting the
mightiness of the continuous, supernatural intervention of God.
Then, just as the widow in 2 Kings became an illustration of
the power of her God to step out of heaven and into her circumstances, we can be the occasion in our world of God's stepping
out of heaven and revealing himself in century twenty! What
this world needs is a fresh unveiling of the almightiness of God!
I have a feeling that he has moved in the circumstances of this
century to bring us to the greatest hour of need the church has
ever known. Why? So he might prove himself Deliverer in our
generation. When we have expended our last resource, retired
our last gimmick, dismissed our last human hope, and cry, "Alas,
Lord, our hope is in you!" then God will step forward. God's
plan of economy works like that . . . DEMAND, DESPERA-
TION, DEPENDENCE, and then DELIVERANCE.

4
THREE POWERFUL PROPOSITIONS

"O depth of wealth, wisdom, and knowledge in God! How unsearchable his judgments, how untraceable his ways! Who knows the mind of the Lord? Who has been his counsellor? Who has ever made a gift to him, to receive a gift in return? Source, Guide, and Goal of all that is—to him be glory for ever! Amen!" (Rom. 11:33-36, NEB).

These three designations form the bases on which the whole issue rests. The principles of a previous chapter presume upon the truth of these claims for their validity. I want you to see some of the implications of these claims before we investigate them more fully concerning our response to them. All reality is bound up in God. If we were standing on the banks of a mighty river named *Reality,* we could say that it flowed from God—he is its *source;* we could say that it flowed through God—he is its *force;* and we could say that it flows to God—he is its *course.*

He is the *derivation,* the *destination,* and the *dynamic* of all that is! That is, everything comes from him (*derivation*); everything moves toward him (*destination*); and everything operates through him (*dynamic*). But this is not mere philosophy and rhetoric, it is powerful, personal, and practical truth to which we must respond. We shall deal with each of these claims within the framework of PROPOSITION and RESPONSE.

PROPOSITION ONE: GOD IS THE DERIVATION OF ALL THAT IS.
Response to Proposition: I choose to recognize that every manifestation of earthly reality is derived from God. I affirm that he is the ground of all reality. All things are in him, and by him all things consist. I now designate him as the total source of my supply. I can never know a need beyond his dynamic

to fulfill. I yield to him the government of all my affairs.

This is precisely the farthest point of the response to this claim. Since he is the source of all things, all things come from him; we must take practical measures to make our lives consistent with this fact. We must not only recognize but respond accordingly to the last practical detail in our lives. Our whole plan of economy must be launched from this platform. It is unfortunate that there is a chapter division after verse 36 in Romans 11. The next statement says, "Therefore, my brothers, I implore you by God's mercy to offer your very selves to him: a living sacrifice, dedicated and fit for his acceptance, the worship offered by mind and heart. Adapt yourselves no longer to the pattern of this present world, but let your minds be remade and your whole nature thus transformed. Then you will be able to discern the will of God, and to know what is good, acceptable, and perfect" (Rom. 12:1-2, NEB).

Thus, in response to the fact that all things come from God, we must make a present of ourselves to him, allowing the rules of the spirit world to transform us from the mold of this present world. We must make available to him not only our total possessions and resources but also our very selves, our bodies in which we in our totality reside. At the precise moment we make all that we are available to him, he makes all that he is available to and through us, not just to meet our needs but to meet the needs of others through us! His economy begins, thus, to operate as do we in his economy. His being the DERIVATION is the point of INITIATION of this eternal plan of economy, and my response is one of PRESENTATION of all that I am and have to him.

PROPOSITION TWO: GOD IS THE DESTINATION OF ALL THAT IS.

Response to Proposition: In the light of the fact that God is the goal of all that is, I choose to make his *glory* my only *goal*. As I live, I will live unto him. As I give, I will give unto him.

I choose to designate him as my only objective in living, service, and giving. In him I will live, and love, and have my being.

If we are to live a life of eternal reality, we must find the direction in which eternal reality is flowing. We must find which way God is moving and move with him. Otherwise, we shall miss the whole point and purpose of life. Life came from him, and life is going back to him.

The Bible leaves no doubt about what God is doing in regard to our world. He has proposed that in the dispensation of the fullness of time he might gather together in Christ all things both which are in heaven and which are on earth (Eph. 1:10). That is our destination. This is where we are headed. This is what salvation is all about. We are redeemed to reverse directions so that we might move toward him. The end is that we might be to the praise of his glory.

Paul must have found this secret when he said, "And whatsoever ye do in word or deed, do all in the name of the Lord Jesus, giving thanks to God and the Father by him" (Col. 3:17). The sole motivation for service is to please the Lord. He further said, "and whatsoever ye do, do it heartily as to the Lord, and not unto men; knowing that of the Lord ye shall receive the reward of the inheritance: for ye serve the Lord Christ" (Col. 3:23). This is our lot: living life facing him, always headed toward home and him! His being the DESTINATION is the point of CONSUMMATION in this eternal plan of economy, and my response is one of CONCENTRATION of all my appetites, affections, and aspirations on him!

PROPOSITION THREE: GOD IS THE DYNAMIC OF ALL THAT IS.

Response to Proposition: I choose to rely entirely upon God for the dynamic to live my life, having named him as my source and destination. He is not only the *source from* which all reality *flows* and the *destination* to which all reality *flows* but he is also the *means* and *might by* which all reality flows.

That God is the *derivation* of all that is settles the mystery of the *past;* that God is the *destination* of all that is settles the mystery of the *future;* that God is the *dynamic* of all that is settles the mystery of the *present.*

We, thus, draw *from* him in order to give *to* him, and in the entire process live *by* him. He settles the matter of directions in our lives.

Jesus in his life and ministry provides a model in which these propositions are put on exhibit. He knew from whence he came: He came from the Father. He made it clear that he had been sent of the Father. He knew his source. He had settled the issue of his derivation.

He knew where he was going. "I go to my Father." In John 13 he is recorded as knowing that the hour had come when he should depart out of this world *unto* the Father. He had settled the matter of his destination. Once we have settled the matter of our destination, the trip seems easier, regardless of where we might be forced to spend time on the way.

He recognized the means which moved his life toward the goal. "The Father who dwells in me, He does the work!"

SOURCE, GOAL, AND GUIDE!!! Thus is God's designation to us. He is the beginning, the end, and all in between. He is the entrance, end, and energy of life.

His being the DYNAMIC of all that is seals the fact of CON-TINUATION in the eternal plan of economy, and my response is CONFIDENCE.

All of this simply means that by engaging these three powerful propositions, we have moved into the dimension of an economy transcendent to that of this world in which unlimited resources are waiting to be tapped. We have chosen to unite the totality of our humanity with the eternal purposes of Deity. We have chosen to admit and affirm that we are children of eternity and not time. Here we stand with resources as rich as heaven and energy as limitless as God.

"Herein is our love made perfect, that we may have boldness

in the day of judgment: because as he is, so are we in this world"
(1 John 4:17). We are a part of his plan because we are a part
of his person! Jesus promised, "At that day ye shall know that
I am in my Father, and ye in me, and I in you" (John 14:20).

THE FALL AND THE CALL

It is here that it becomes clear that in the fall of man in
the garden, man became a drop-out in God's plan of economy.
He forfeited his right to fit into his role in reflecting the glory
of God. He literally fell out of God's cycle of life. Praise the
Lord that the fall was not final. God pursued man with a call
to salvation. That salvation restores man to his intended humanity, in order that God in his Deity may so inhabit that humanity
as to involve man again in His plan of economy.

5
THE PERSON OF CHRIST AND THE PLAN OF GOD

"The life and ministry of Jesus presents a clear exhibit of the pattern and power of God's plan of economy. In our redemption, Jesus provides for us the relationship which was his with the Father. As we are prepared to be to him all that he was to the Father, he is prepared to be all to us that the Father was to him."　　　　　　　　　　　　　　　—Selected

Nowhere in the universe is there a better model of the worth and workability of God's plan of economy than in the person of Christ. His life is a record of complete obedience to principles which govern life in the spirit dimension, and yet he lived in a normal human body. As the Second Adam he demonstrated the power and purpose of God as decidedly as the First Adam had defaulted to the devil. We are going to examine in this chapter the four-fold secret of Jesus in relationship to the plan of God.

Jesus had a secret as he lived in this world. That secret formulated the dynamic by which he was to live and in which he ministered. It is through observing the qualities of that secret that we become acquainted with the arrangement of God for us to live life to the fullest in the purpose of his economy. As we observe the facets of that secret, I challenge you to compare the relationship he had with the Father with the relationship he has made available to us through his death and resurrection life. You will have, thus, discovered a key to the implementation of the plan of God for you.

FIRST: JESUS WAS BORN OF THE FATHER.

A strange birth announcement: "The Holy Ghost shall come upon thee, and the power of the Highest shall overshadow thee: therefore that holy thing which shall be born of thee shall be

55

called the Son of God" (Luke 1:35). This was the announcement of the one and only *virgin birth*. The term never would have been coined had it not been for Jesus. It is an incompatible, an impossible fact! Yet, with God all things are possible. There is much doubt and discussion in theological circles as to the virgin birth. There is no doubt in the Bible! Matthew's Gospel records that "she was found with child by the Holy Ghost" (Matt. 1:18). This fact was further confirmed by the visitation of the angel who announced, "That which is conceived in her is of the Holy Ghost" (Matt. 1:20). Isaiah had prophesied a long time ago, saying, "Behold, a *virgin* shall conceive, and bear a son" (Isa. 7:14).

The angel Gabriel came to Mary and said, "Hail, thou art highly favoured, the Lord is with thee: blessed art thou among women" (Luke 1:28). It is highly unlikely that the angel would have had such commending words to a woman who had been guilty of premarital sex, a crime which merited death in the Old Testament! Besides all this, the verses just prior to that designated her twice as a virgin. "And in the sixth month the angel Gabriel was sent from God unto a city of Galilee, named Nazareth, to a *virgin* espoused to a man whose name was Joseph, of the house of David; and the *virgin's* name was Mary" (Luke 1:26-27).

John called him the "Word made flesh" saying, "He dwelt among us, (and we beheld his glory, the glory as of the *only begotten* of the Father,) full of grace and truth" (John 1:14). He was begotten of the Father. Jesus confirmed this when he said, "For God so loved the world, that he gave his only begotten Son" (John 3:16).

The fact is that Jesus had to be born as he was born to be what he was, to do what he did. He was not just a man. He was more than man. He was man plus God. That is why he was who he was! That is why he was able to do what he did. There is simply no other explanation.

There are some theologians who deny the virgin birth, and they are joined by others who say it really doesn't matter. If Jesus was not virgin-born, he was an illegitimate child. If he was an illegitimate child, the Bible is mistaken, the angel was deceived, and Jesus was either a lunatic or a liar. If he had a human father, he was of the nature of fallen Adam and, thus, disqualified to be Savior. But his being virgin-born was the foundation of his secret. He had come from the Father. Though he had a human body, he was inhabited by God. He was a man plus God.

That same secret is ours as believers. We, too, have been born of the Father. We who have been saved have had a very remarkable thing happen to us. We have been born of the Spirit with life from above. The life of God has entered us by the Spirit. We are inhabited by Deity! Every one of us is a person plus God. We have been rendered supernatural. Just as the supernatural birth of Jesus qualified him for God's plan of economy, our supernatural birth qualifies us for that same plan. The moment we were born again, we were equipped to live in that other dimension which is transcendent to the sense world. We became children of another economy . . . a supernatural plan for a supernatural life. So, we are qualified to live in the spirit world by being born the second time. As Jesus was related to the Father, so are we related to the Father through him. As he is, so are we in the world. This is not some mystical theory but a present, practical reality.

Being born again, you have become a candidate for the conquering life. Determine to abide by the stated rules of the dimension of the spirit, and victory will be yours! What he is, you are. What he has, you have. His life is yours. His life in you is the *hope of glory.* The hope of glory is that you will become all that you were made to be. The only hope of realizing that is JESUS LIVING IN YOU. That began the moment you were born again!

SECOND: HE WAS COMMITTED TO DO THE FATHER'S WILL.

The second facet of the secret of Jesus was that his sole purpose was bound up in the purpose of God. The subject came up when his disciples inquired where he had gotten nourishment. He replied that he had meat to eat that they knew not of. He was not talking in sense-world terms but in spirit-world terms. He had spirit-world food for spirit-world work. He was physical, as physical as any of his disciples, but his relationship with God and obedience to God's order caused the spiritual to dominate the physical. The physical was subject to the spiritual. He then revealed the second facet of his secret: "My meat is to do the will of him that sent me, and to finish his work" (John 4:34).

He was confessing that his source of sustenance was the motivation to do God's will. He was exclusively committed to be identified with the work of God. He had no plan apart from God's and sought no other power than God's in which to do His work. His reason for existence was inextricably bound up in the redemptive plan of God. He had come to finish God's work!

Jesus was here on business! He would not be deterred or distracted. His face was set. His meat and drink was to do the Father's will. This was the sustaining force within his life!

No less are you and I on business here! Jesus informed his own that as the Father had sent him, we were being sent. That little word *as* joins us to his purpose and power. The arrangements are the same. Just as God lived in Jesus to do his will, so Jesus lives in us to do the will of the Father. In such an arrangement, Jesus had all the resources of God at his disposal. Thus do we have, through Jesus' indwelling us, the entirety of God's resources open and available to us. Just as Jesus had more to give than he possessed as a mere human being, so do you and I have more to give than humanity has.

We have supernatural power for supernatural work. It is pitiful when we depend upon human machinery and human energy to seek to do the eternal work of redeeming mankind!

Jesus was *committed* to the Father, *identified* with the Father, and *available* to the Father. Being such he was to God a human body so completely belonging to God that God was obliged to occupy that humanity so completely and control that humanity so thoroughly that he could do *what* he desired, *where* he desired, *when* he desired, regardless of the circumstances. And to repeat the words with which this chapter began . . . *When you are prepared to be to Jesus what Jesus was to the Father, Jesus is prepared to be to you what the Father was to him.* So, you have the terms of a supernatural economy right here in this world: God dwelling in a man's humanity, so completely in control of that humanity that he can extend himself through that available humanity to any spot on the earth.

THIRD: HE DID WHAT HE SAW THE FATHER DOING.

It is here that Jesus divulges a startling secret. He says, "The Son can do nothing of himself" (John 5:19). Now, isn't that startling? That really isn't what a leader is supposed to say in the presence of his followers! He is supposed to exhibit and exude confidence. But here Jesus admits that he doesn't have it! I believe that this is as much a part of his secret as the recognition of his resources. He would not have lived reliant on divine resources if somewhere along the line he had become convinced of his adequacy as a mere human being. To preface the next facet of his secret, he repeated a similar affirmation: "I can of mine own self do nothing" (John 5:30). He was simply stating that he had no power or plan outside of the Father. Oh, he was able as a human being, but that was not enough for life in that other dimension. You and I can develop our human abilities to a keen edge but still have no effectiveness in the spirit realm.

If Jesus were able to state it rather forthrightly, why should it break my jaw to say it . . . "I can't do it! I don't have it!" He never would have had an occasion for watching what the Father was doing had he had "plans of his own." But since he had come from the Father and was committed to the Father, it was reasonable that he look to the Father only and always for what he was to do. Thus, he said, "My Father worketh hitherto, and I work" (John 5:17). He further stated, "The Son can do nothing of himself, but what he seeth the Father do: for what things soever he doeth, these also doeth the Son likewise. For the Father loveth the Son, and sheweth him all things that himself doeth" (John 5:19-20). Jesus had double vision. He had 20-20 vision in the sense world, but he also had perfect vision in the spirit realm. He never allowed what he saw in the former to dominate what he saw in the latter.

FOURTH: JESUS SAID WHAT HE HEARD THE FATHER SAYING.

Just as Jesus had double vision, he had double hearing. He could hear in the sense realm, but he could also hear in the spirit realm. He never let what he heard in the sense realm overrule what he heard in the spirit realm. He was always listening to what God had to say. He said, "As I hear, I judge; and my judgment is just; because I seek not mine own will, but the will of the Father which hath sent me" (John 5:30). In the next verse Jesus said, "If I bear witness of myself, my witness is not true" (John 5:31). Jesus here confesses that if he registered his own judgment, it would not hold good! Imagine that! As perfect as was his humanity, he still could not rely on it. How much less can we rely on the best of our fallen humanity for right judgment!

Now this is beautiful if you can see it. Let's put those two facets together and see if we cannot illustrate the plan more evidently. Stating this two-fold arrangement as one: *He did what he saw and said what he heard.* The result was that he was never guilty of saying or doing the wrong thing. He always did the right things, and he always said the right things! The secret was that *he didn't do until he saw and he didn't say until he heard!* If he didn't see, he stayed still; if he didn't hear, he stayed silent. He had eyes and ears open to that other dimension which is eternal. He moved only when he saw God move and spoke only when he heard God speak.

Now, an illustration. Jesus always reckoned a situation as a call to watch and listen to the Father. He was always encountering situations. One day he preached to a large multitude of people. There were at least 5,000 men. Women and children could have caused the crowd to swell to 15,000 or 20,000. But a problem (?) developed. I insert the question mark because Jesus saw problems, not as problems but as opportunities to pull his disciples into the spirit realm and let them see the God of heaven in action in the earth. They were often dull and missed the point, though they usually were around when the glory came.

The problem was that the people were hungry, it being mealtime, and there was virtually nothing for them to eat. On the human side, it was indeed a problem. There was no doubt about that! Now watch Jesus. Remember that he is witness to two worlds, the spirit world and the sense world. And for a time those two worlds stand facing each other. The disciples looked only upon the sense world. Jesus looked at the crowd with his physical eyes and asked Philip, "Whence shall we buy bread, that these may eat?" Then the Holy Spirit inserted this revelation, "And this he said to prove him: for he himself knew what he would do" (John 6:5-6). The last statement demonstrated that he had also peered into that other world and had seen what God was up to.

But alas, Philip failed the test. He gave an answer from conclusions drawn from his own common sense. He gave the same answer any self-respecting atheist would give! "Lord, it would take a year's salary to feed this crowd!" What he was really saying was that it was totally impossible. About that time up came Andrew with a little lad tugging at his coat. If his first statement was a statement of faith, his second statement cancelled it. "There is a lad here, which hath five barley loaves, and two small fishes: (he should have stopped there!) but what are they among so many?" (John 6:9). He was still reckoning human resources for human problems. That was his mistake. He had not taken heaven into account.

But Jesus lived in such unbroken communication with the Father that no situation was a cause for alarm. He simply watched and listened, and then moved. He knew what he would do, because he knew what the Father was doing. When he saw what was going on in heaven with regard to that situation, he simply prayed heaven down to earth! He saw the thousands of milling, hungry people, but he also saw the unlimited resources of the heavenly bakery and fish market! He gave a command, gave thanks, distributed to the disciples, and one dimension invaded another with unseen resources becoming visible . . . and the crowd was filled! Unusual? Yes, from the standpoint of the sense world but quite normal from the standpoint of the spirit world! The folks were not only well fed, but there was a solid surplus! Jesus had exhibited the economy of the spirit dimension!

Now our chief problem is that most of our activity is in accord with what our human eyes have seen and what our human ears have heard. Most of our programs are cast along this line. We seldom watch for God or listen to what he is saying. We are too busy doing our own thing, or as we often say, "doing great things for him." We have not developed our spirit-world eyes and ears to behold what God is up to and, thus, are insensitive when we should be sensitive. Opportunities come and go for us to get God in on our circumstances, and we miss it like Philip would have and Andrew! It might be a good rule to say, "If you haven't seen God doing it, *shut down!* If you haven't heard God saying it, *shut up!*

The supreme dynamic of the Christian life is the indwelling of Christ in the life of the believer. He is in us. He is all that he is in heaven in us. We will not have anymore of Jesus in us in heaven than we do right at this moment. The words should be constantly ringing in our ears, "and I in you" (John 15:4). He in us is our pass key into the world of God's miraculous economy. God's plan of economy goes on, because Jesus is still alive in every one of his followers. And to all who are willing to have him be sum and substance of their lives, that divine economy can be real daily.

His secret is our secret!

He was born of the Father. So we have been born again.

He was committed to do the Father's will. So we can be committed to do the Father's will.

His doing was according to the Father's. So we can see what God is up to in his behalf in our circumstances and move in cooperation with him.

He was always saying what he heard the Father say. So I can know what God has said and speak, "Thus saith the Lord!"

THE NECESSITY OF THE HIDDEN LIFE

It seems and sounds rather simple that all the Christian has to do is see what God is up to and get in on it. It must be said that as simple as it sounds, and as simply as it was demonstrated in the life and ministry of Jesus, there is one master secret behind it all. *That is the hidden life of communication with God.* This is the great lack of our day! If we spend our time counseling with the flesh, we shall do the will of the flesh. We take on the aspects of that with which we have communion. Flesh communes with flesh, and spirit with spirit. Anyone can see God's *acts*. It takes intimate communion to know God's *ways*. The rank and file of the Israelites could see the *acts* of God. Hours upon hours in deep communion with God qualified Moses to know God's *ways*. "He made known his ways unto Moses, his acts unto the children of Israel" (Ps. 103:7). It is in the hidden life that we develop faith which "gives substance to our hopes, and makes us certain of realities we do not see" (Heb. 11:1, NEB). We can expect no more dividends to accrue to our citizenship in heaven than are commensurate to the time and energy we spend in the hidden place with God. We must develop the art of watching God and listening to God. We must know when he is in the wings waiting to come in. We must develop the art of sensing when he is glad or grieved, ready or reticent. This can only be done in the hidden place. Hours of fellowship with our beloved brothers may gladden our hearts temporarily and improve our standing among our peers, but it does not do much for developing the dimensions of the spirit.

We must return to the hidden place to implement the secret of Jesus. Our *union* will never mean any more than our *communion*. Our *relationship* with God will have no more dynamic than does our *fellowship* with him. In this, too, our secret is that we have Jesus in us as our life. His life in us is a praying life, a meditating life, a God-seeking life.

Hear what Andrew Murray says in the introduction to his volume, *With Christ In The School Of Prayer:* "Of all the promises connected with the command, ABIDE IN ME, there is none higher, and none that sooner brings the confession, 'Not that I had already attained, or am already made perfect,' than this: 'If ye abide in me and I in you, ye shall ask whatsoever you will, and it shall be done unto you.' Power with God is the highest attainment of the life of full abiding."

And we know that abiding is impossible without great attention to the hidden life. We may know the secrets of God's economy, even be able to expound on them, but unless we are implementing them in the secret place with God, it will be so much knowledge without power.

The world waits for a church, a group of people . . . ordinary people who have discovered an extraordinary truth . . . namely, that Jesus lives in them and is totally available to them as they make themselves available to him. These moving from the secret circle of communion with God to tasks to which God and heaven are committed . . . there will be stirrings in the tops of the mulberries. And soon God will make his glory known among the heathen.

6

THE PROGRAM IN A WORD

Note: This chapter deserves your most serious consideration. To this point we have been viewing, investigating, observing claims. From this point and especially in this chapter we will be reacting to truth. God's glorious plan will become reality in your life or pass on by according to what you do with the truth in these following pages. Read prayerfully, thoroughly, and, if needed, repeatedly.

THE WORD PRESENTED

Every now and then there is word in the Word of God so inclusive, so exclusive, so fitting that it is appropriate—in every circumstance to every person who will listen and apply. It can be believed and put into action in any and every circumstance, and the results will be astounding. It can be believed by the lost, and they will, when it is applied, be saved. It can be believed by the saved, and they will come to a new expression of spiritual reality in their own lives.

It can be taken by the lonely, and the result will be the cure of loneliness. It is relevant in every situation for every person. If revival is the need, the truth which comes with this word will bring revival. When put into practice, it will open the hearts of people and the windows of heaven as well. Avenues of communication, clogged with misunderstanding, will once again flow with rushing streams of gladness. If life has become dull and spiritless, the suggestion of this word will inject new excitement into any life. It will work at any level and at any age.

John D. Rockefeller was dying at age fifty-five! He was living on crackers and milk and could scarcely enjoy the results of his untold wealth. He spent most of his time in bed, but at his own word had not enjoyed one uninterrupted hour of sleep in five years! He was hungry but could not eat, miserable with no apparent recourse but to slowly give in to death. He was weakened by a blood disease and racked with pain from an ulcerated stomach. He supposed that since he was going to die, he might enjoy doing something that he had not done until then. Among the things he did, there was one activity which he credited with much of his miraculous healing! He lived after that thirty-five more years! What was that one thing? HE LEARNED TO *GIVE!* Within twelve months after he began the exciting adventure of giving, he was virtually well and spent the rest of his days a whole man!

The word is GIVE! It is a word so simple that it really requires no definition. Give this word to a child who has never been to school, and the chances are real that he will understand what it means. It is a simple four-letter word that exists in a day when four-letter words have fallen upon hard times. There are many good four-letter words, however. L-O-V-E is one of them. W-O-R-K is another! This is another . . . G-I-V-E! The word is a complete sentence in itself. The subject and remainder of the predicate are understood.

We meet this word most memorably in Luke 6:38. Since you may know it by memory, allow me to give you the Amplified Version: "Give and gifts will be given you, good measure, pressed down, shaken together, and running over will they pour into the pouch formed by the bosom of your robe and used as a bag. For with the measure you deal out . . . that is, with the measure you use when you confer benefits on others . . . it will be measured unto you again."

What a fantastic statement! And the more you know and the more you apply it, the more fantastic it will seem! I want to examine the structure and content of that verse with you. It actually contains three component parts: First, a *command:* "Give!" Second, a *promise:* "And it shall be given unto you." Third, a *principle:* The same measure you use will be used with you.

This is God's plan in a word. The whole sentence hinges on the first word—GIVE! The rest is simply an explanation of that activity and the results. I call it sometimes—revival in a word! It is the shortest route to glory!

Do you find yourself in circumstances in which you had rather not be? Are you experiencing deficiencies in every area of life? Have you just about tried it all? Then try this! I want you to observe four things with me about this splendid word from the lips of Jesus. First, it is a personal word. Second, it is a practical word. Third, it is a possible word. Fourth, it is a profitable word.

FIRST: IT IS A PERSONAL WORD.

It is personally *inclusive.* The command is plural, as is evidenced in the Greek. Thus, this is for *everybody.* Not only this, but it is inclusive of *everything.* There is no doubt left as to *who* is supposed to give. The answer is simply EVERYONE. Now, there is equally no doubt as to what is supposed to be given. The absence of a specification demands a general implication. You say, "So I am supposed to give but *what* am I supposed to give?" The answer is EVERYTHING! We have already said that stewardship includes all commodities of life. I will have a suggestion later concerning where you should choose to start your giving program. The command to give includes all that we are and have, or will ever be or have.

It is personally *imperative.* There is a mood in every language that speaks of necessity—demand! It is called the *imperative* mood. It implies that there is no option. It is a clear demand. Some words declare facts. The imperative demands response.

Once accosted by an imperative, you cannot hear it and go away ever expecting to be the same.

It is personally *continuous*. The word in the Greek is in the present tense which has a *continuous* connotation. It can be properly read in the English, "You all must be always continuously giving." Giving does not stop with an act. It becomes an attitude and an unceasing demonstration. Jesus was really saying, "Let giving be your permanent life-style!"

It is personally *unconditional*. There is no "if" before or after this command. That means that it is conditioned upon nothing. There are no contingencies, no loopholes, no excluding clauses, no disqualifying addenda. Nobody can reply, "But I have nothing to give!"

Thus, the command to give is to everyone, regarding everything continuously, without conditions!

SECOND: IT IS A PRACTICAL WORD.

Within that one little word is the key to the mysteries of the universe. There is a law written within the context of the universe that, when applied and adhered to, will release the riches of the whole system. When that law is broken or disregarded, the whole system of reality seems to lock up around us.

It is practical in *nature*. Look at the benevolent system of nature. There is a mutual sharing within the context of nature. Investigate the mysteries of the *tree*. It exists to produce. The whole of its system revolves around the ultimate intention to *give*. It draws from the depths of the soil and from the air those qualities needed to produce fruit. It does this without prodding or pushing. Look at the *earth* itself. There is life within the earth, life to be given. Plant a tree or seed in that earth, and it will burst into life. This occurs and continues to occur through an intricate network of unseen but vital, cooperative forces within nature. All this goes on while we are awake and while we sleep, seedtime and harvest!

Look at the *sun*. For ages and ages it has been giving from its vast resources of energy and is itself a giver of energy. Vitamin C is a vital source of health to humankind. It comes as a result of sunshine. Stand out in the sun today, and you will feel its life-giving rays warming the atmosphere. It is giving! You are taking.

If you are to be a part of this benevolent cycle of the universe you must give, or the cycle will be broken with you. Look at the *seed*. Now here is a marvel! Man can duplicate it almost to perfection with one exception—man cannot create life. There is life within that seed. A tiny little particle is imprisoned within the walls of that seed. I am told that such life can be imprisoned for hundreds of years and still be vital. But that life is useless imprisoned thusly. Let that seed by given to multiply, to be fruitful, and a miracle results. It is placed in the dark ground and covered over. But if we could watch and understand, we would see several things occur. We would see it break, literally burst open in order that the inner life may be expressed. Then tiny *roots* would be sent down for nourishment to this new life. Then tiny *shoots* would go up toward the sun, bursting through the topsoil in due time. In this process I am informed that all the starch in the little seed turns to sugar! (Could be a key to getting the starch out of many of us!) All this because of giving! It is practical in nature. You sat down to eat today because someone and something practiced the power of giving!

It is practical, not only in nature, but in *human need*. I previously mentioned that I would suggest a place for you to begin your giving program. That is now what I will do, and I promise you that you are going to be surprised. And your surprise will be a source of much learning if you will so allow! On the basis of this command of Jesus, I confess to you that the place to begin your giving is in *that place where you are now experiencing your greatest present need*.

Now, before you protest let me remind you of the substance of what Jesus said. He said that we were to give and that we could expect to receive more than we gave! To accentuate that promise, he used four descriptives to suggest how much more! First, he said "good measure" which means literally "a good, precious, or honorable quantity." Second, he said "pressed down" which in the Greek is in the rare, but reflective, perfect tense and can be rendered here "perfectly and permanently satisfied"! Third, he said "shaken together," another perfect word to denote a permanent and perfect work, which literally means "to unsettle." (The obvious purpose here is to make for more room.) Fourth, Jesus said "running over" which means "continuously pouring out." *Thus, the promise to the giver is that he will receive.*

Now, what if you are experiencing an unmet need? Let me suggest an answer . . . *either Jesus misrepresented the truth or you have a giving problem!* Jesus promised ample receiving with giving. If we are not receiving, then something is wrong. We can do away with the first possibility. Jesus never misrepresents the truth, *he is the truth!* Then you must have a giving problem! Now, I realize that this does not make sense to the human senses, but this shouldn't give us any problem. God's ways are not our ways, nor his thoughts our thoughts.

I am going to suggest a couple of areas where you might begin to demonstrate the power of this principle of giving. Let's suppose that you are one of those people who never seems to have enough time. You often wish for more hours in the day and more days in the week. The weeks and months and years speed by, and you never seem to be able to get everything done that you plan to do. You unconsciously accuse God of being unwise in creating days as short as they seem to be! Oh, for more time! Your cry constantly is, "Oh, how I need more time!" Well, you will never have more time. It can't be saved and must be spent, and along with everything else, you will give account for how time was spent.

I come to suggest that if you never seem to have all the time you need and are frustrated about it, you have a giving problem regarding time. In short, you are not giving enough time away. Let me make a specific suggestion or two. First, deliberately give God more time the first thing in the morning. You might have to rise that much earlier, but your strength will be ample to do it. God will see to that. Second, in the midst of your busy day, seek someone out who has need and give them some of the most precious commodity you have—time! If the promise of Jesus is valid (and who would doubt that?), you will seem to have more time, because the providence of God will begin to operate on your priorities and energy to make it seem that he has actually added hours to your days. *Try it—you'll like it!*

Again, I suggest that you choose another area of your life where you are constantly experiencing deficiency. A common area would be in the vicinity of physical energy. Are you tired, simply drained of all apparent energy? Let me suggest a simple experiment to prove that this principle of giving works in the physical realm as in the spiritual realm. In your state of apparent fatigue, deliberately engage in a few minutes of semistrenuous exercise according to your general physical condition. You may want to run in place, jog around the block, do sit-ups, do push-ups, or simply jump up and down a few dozen times. Follow this up with a warm shower, allowing the water to get cool to end the shower. I can guarantee you almost without exception that you will experience a revival of energy within moments. If your physical condition renders this an unwise suggestion, you have enough truth to contrive an experiment of your own!

Giving is the *practical* thing to do! Start giving at the point of your greatest need!

THIRD: IT IS A PERSONALLY POSSIBLE WORD.

Here is a command well within the reach of every person alive. You see, God never gave a command to man beyond man's capacity to obey. Thus, EVERY COMMAND WAS AT ONCE A PROMISE. If God commanded it, then God always enables what he commands. None of us can excuse ourselves and go away. I recall for you some illustrations from the Word of God.

When Jesus, standing outside the tomb of Lazarus, said, "Lazarus, come forth!" (John 11:43), Lazarus didn't say, "I can't Lord, I've been dead four days!" He came forth. He wasn't even dressed for the occasion of life. He was dressed for death. Have you ever considered how he got there to the mouth of the tomb? He was bound—head, foot, hand, and face—but he got there! What Jesus commanded, he enabled! Praise the Lord!

One day Jesus was teaching in the synagogue, and there came in a man with a withered hand. Jesus stopped his teaching and said, "Stretch forth thine hand!" (Matt. 12:13; Mark 3:5; Luke 6:10). The man didn't stand there and say, "You wouldn't mock a cripple, would you? I cannot stretch forth my hand!" No, he stretched it forth. Jesus enabled what he commanded. What he states as *imperative* is not *impossible*.

There was the lame man who had residence on the same pallet for thirty-eight years (John 5:5-9). One day Jesus came by and said, "Rise, take up thy bed, and walk." That man didn't say, "I can't. I've tried a thousand times, but I can't!" He did it! He did just what Jesus commanded him to do. He found that anything Jesus demanded was backed by His dynamic! His command was a promise!

Aren't you glad that he never asks us to do something that we cannot do? Thus, we should never be shocked at any command. The fact that Jesus makes the command is the statement of the promise that we have in us in him the power to perform it! Hallelujah!

FOURTH: IT IS A PERSONALLY PROFITABLE WORD.

This is not at all sensible to the human mind. But it is true! This is one of the planks in the platform of God's plan of economy. It is profitable to give God's way.

Look at the *promise*. It is a careful promise that Jesus makes here, "Give, and it shall be given unto you" (Luke 6:38). It shall be. Remember that Jesus said that he only repeated what he heard the Father say. John 5:30 says, "As I hear, I judge, and my judgment is just." He would not have made the promise had he known for sure that the resources of the Father would not be available to back it up! Notice that the source will be "men" . . . "Shall men give into your bosom" (Luke 6:38). My first thought, when I first read this, was: "But, what if God cannot find enough men willing to give?" And the thought followed, "He will knock it out of them and still get it for me to keep his promise!" I needn't be concerned about his end of the bargain, only mine, and mine is to GIVE! We will always discover that it is profitable. The four descriptives about which we have already talked denote *endless supply, permanent conditions of plenty,* and *continuous overflow.*

The figure used here suggests great magnitude. "Into your bosom" is better translated "into your lap." In those days men wore long, flowing robes. If a man reached as far down as possible with both hands and drew the reaches of his garment up and back toward his head, he would create a fold with his garment which would have great capacity. This is perhaps what Jesus did as he spoke in this manner. I can envision him in my imagination talking excitedly and drawing his garment up into a great cup of capacity saying, "A man who gives shall receive this much!"

Look next at the *principle.* Everyone is living proof of the truth of this principle. *The measure of your getting will be in proportion to your giving!* This is an eternal invariable! This is a law written within nature as certain as the law of gravity. One cannot break it as much as he breaks himself upon it. The same measure you use in giving to others will be used in giving to you. The God of the universe promises that. Paul backs this up as he states in 2 Corinthians 9:6: "But this I say, he which soweth sparingly shall reap also sparingly; and he which sows bountifully shall reap also bountifully."

Now, remember that this is a principle! It is not a suggestion that *might* come to pass. It will always happen! Sow sparingly and you will reap sparingly—always! Sow bountifully and you will reap bountifully—always! How much you receive rests with you. The widow in Elisha's ministry limited her receiving only by the degree of her obedience in preparing to receive. *Giving is a profitable adventure!*

CONCLUSIONS

There are some basic conclusions that we can declare from our study of this verse. We can expect from our giving to receive. We can expect from our giving to receive more than we give. The absence of a qualified limit would lead us to believe that there is absolutely no limit. That is further strengthened by the fact that we believe our God is a God of *unlimited resources.* Then, God has given us a mighty gift—the privilege of giving! With that privilege exercised, we can open the treasures of the whole universe and get heaven down to earth. We can move God into the affairs of men! We can cause God's eternal plan of economy to invade the realms of earth and make a difference in hundreds and thousands of lives.

The most obvious conclusion of all is simply this: GIVE! Give of that commodity which you seem to have the least of, where you are experiencing your greatest need. If you lack love, seek to give more love away, and there will be love bestowed upon you in abundance. If you lack time, try giving more time away to God and man. God's gift to you will be released time to do what you should do! If others seem unconcerned for you, give away concern, lavish concern on those with no view to what they can do for you. The result is guaranteed! Jesus promises that you will receive.

Here is a closing word of warning. Though we can give, knowing of the promise of Jesus that we shall receive, that receiving is never the motive for our giving. We give to give more! Thus, what we are to get, because we have given, is to be given, and the cycle is go on and on and on. We are to give to get to give to get to give . . . ad infinitum! The conclusion: GIVE, GIVE, GIVE, GIVE!!!

7
GOD'S CYCLE OF SUFFICIENCY

"And God is able to make all grace, every favor and earthly blessing come to you in abundance, so that you may always and under all circumstances and whatever the need, be self-sufficient . . . possessing enough to require no aid or support and furnished in abundance for every good work and charitable donation"
(2 Cor. 9:8, *Amplified*).

I want to introduce to you a concept which has become a source of great joy to me. I call it God's cycle of sufficiency. I have always loved 2 Corinthians 9:8. It is one of those verses which is fitting in or out of context. It goes full circle from God's ability, sweeps down to man—through man—to meet needs that all good works demand, and back again to the glory of God where it all began. I want you to see it not just for the *pleasure of perusing* it, but for the *prosperity of participating* in it. I do not remember when I have had a verse so capture my imagination as this one has during the past days. Someone is often asking me what my favorite Scripture passage is. My reply is usually, "The one I am just getting ready to preach on!" For this moment this Scripture is my favorite. I pray that during this reading these words will grasp your mind and seize your soul. I pray that when you see what God is up to in His behalf, your determination will be to get in on what he is up to and join the cycle of sufficiency.

GOD'S ABILITY IS THE MIGHT OF IT.

I want you to feature as you read this chapter the drawing of a circle. It will help you envision the cycle of sufficiency as we discuss it. First, start with a point which will be the top of the circle. We shall label this point *God's ability*. This is the point of commencement and the point of consummation.

The whole plan begins and ends with God.

What a way to start a statement—"God is able!" We have already established that all reality has its source in him. In him are stored all the treasures of life's commodities. This is the foundation upon which rests the eternal plan of economy.

When Moses inquired about what answer he should give the people when they asked him who it was that had sent him, God said to tell them that *"I AM* hath sent me unto you!" (Ex. 3:14). He is the "I AM." He is the only being in the whole universe that is safe in saying that. He is eternally "I AM," he was "I AM," he is "I AM," and he always will be "I AM." The cycle of sufficiency is backed up by the name of the One who is in control. No plan of economy is greater, in the ultimate sense, than the total amount of reserves supporting it. Behind this plan there is the name of God, the eternal I AM. His name and resources are the source of sufficiency.

Observe, first, that God's ability is *unqualified.* When God told Moses that His name was to be "I AM," He did not bother to give a predicate to the subject. When God is the subject, the predicate is not needed. Here is the statement *"God is able!"* Though there follows a word that regards the direction of His ability, it is unlimited and unqualified. You could close off the statement with this and be in the truth. He is able. You ask, "Able to do what?" He is able to do anything that is needed. Because he is thus able, there is no need filling up the page with all that he can do. Just wait until you have a need and discover his ability, not as a theory, but as a glad and present reality.

Again, see that God's ability is *unchanging.* Because he is the "I AM"—and that refers to eternal present—his ability is the same yesterday, today, and forever. James informs us that God is One with whom there is neither variableness nor shadow of turning (Js. 1:17). The overwhelming connotation of this is that God's promise today can still be reckoned true in the tomorrows to come. The little word *is* holds yesterday and tomorrow together. God was able yesterday. He will be able tomorrow. He is able today. When I decide to get in on God's plan, I am linking myself with the eternal ability of God.

Never will God depend upon your ability and mine . . . always upon his own. He never expects us to fall back upon our ability. God will do what he must do to keep us depending on his ability. He allowed Paul to have a "messenger of Satan to buffet" (2 Cor. 12:7) him in order that he (Paul) might discover that, in the midst of his own weakness, the power of God would be perfected. God will ever be obliged to drive us back upon our own weakness to keep us next to his strength and glory.

God's ability is the might of the cycle of sufficiency.

ALL GRACE IS THE MEASURE OF IT.

We have begun the circle at the point of God's ability. Now, as you feature the drawing of the circle, move counterclockwise from the starting point of *God's Ability* with a line arching downward labeled *All Grace*. As the line continues downward toward the bottom of the circle, you will begin to see how God's cycle of sufficiency works. Go ahead and feature the words along the circle which Paul uses in our text: "God is able to make all grace abound toward you." From the point of God's ability all grace abounds!

The simple reference here is "all grace." The word for grace literally means "a special manifestation of divine presence, activity, power, or glory." In the strictest sense, the grace of God involves God himself. In giving, he gives himself. The verb form of the word for grace means "to give, or to bestow" or "to deal generously or graciously with." *The New English Bible* translates this: "And it is in God's power to provide you richly with *every good gift*" (2 Cor. 9:8). *The Amplified Version* says, "And God is able to make all grace (every favor and earthly blessing) come to you in abundance . . ."

There is little doubt that "all grace" refers to such a supply that there is no need outside the reaches of its riches. Since

God is the source of our total supply and God owns all the wealth
of every kind in every realm, it is not too much to suppose that
the term "all grace" is an all-inclusive term. We would not be
amiss to say that God's grace involves all God *has,* all God has
done, and all God is!

ABOUNDING IS THE MANNER OF IT.

The abounding cycle continues as the circle moves downward.

Notice that twice within this verse the word *abound* is found.
The word in the Greek means, "increase, abound, overflow, excel,
exceed, have plenty, have more than enough, or to provide in
abundance." Praise the Lord! There is nothing "mere" about
the grace of God. It is always abundant.

The abundance of God is no new concept to the reader of
the Bible. Jesus said, "I am come that they might have life, and
that they might have it more *abundantly.*" (The same form as
used here in 2 Corinthians 9:8 for *abound.*) Look at other references to abounding within this context:

2 Corinthians   8:2: How that in a great trial of affliction the
ABUNDANCE of their joy and their deep
poverty ABOUNDED unto the riches of
their liberality.

8:7: Therefore, as ye ABOUND in every thing,
in faith, and utterance, and knowledge,
and in all diligence, and in your love to
us, see that ye ABOUND in this grace
also. [The grace of giving]

8:14: But by an equality, that now at this time
your ABUNDANCE may be a supply for
their want, that their ABUNDANCE also
may be a supply for your want: that there
may be equality.

8:20: Avoiding this, that no man should blame
us in this ABUNDANCE which is admin-

istered by us.

9:12: For the administration of this service not only supplieth the want of the saints, but is ABUNDANT also by many thanksgivings unto God.

Observe the *source* of that abounding—God's ability.
Observe the *supply* of that abounding—all grace.
Observe the *service* of that abounding—every good work.

While the word *abound* is found twice in the verse, there are five words which speak of abundance—*all* grace, *always*, *all* sufficiency, *all* things, *every* good work.

The reserves behind God's plan of economy are ample!

TOWARD US IS THE MOTION OF IT.

We are discussing here a directed surplus. God's grace is not just abounding but it is abounding TOWARD US. As you move along the circle from the topmost point around toward the bottom, you arrive at the point which we will label *Toward Us*. You now can feature half a circle. The top is *God's Ability*, the bottom, *Toward Us*.

The motion of God's plenty is always "toward us." He is the source, and we are the channel.

OUR ADEQUACY IS THE MEANS OF IT.

At the lowest point of the circle we see ourselves, the objects of his abounding grace. Our thorough adequacy is a necessity in the blessed cycle. You may be certain that all your needs can safely and satisfyingly be brought within the circle, whatever their nature. When someone asks you how much of anything you have, you have an appropriate answer, "Enough!"

Do you remember the much-told story of the Rolls-Royce salesman who was asked by a prospective customer about the total horsepower of the automobile? The salesman did not know, and in turn asked the manager, who himself did not know the answer. Since the answer seemed important to the horse-power-conscious customer, a telegram was sent to the manufacturer in England with the question. In a short time the reply came. There was one word on the reply telegram: "ADEQUATE!" We may say the same thing of our position in Christ with our lives linked to him. Nobody has ever measured the amount of God's ability, nor can it ever be measured, but for your inquiry the answer is always "ADEQUATE!"

Many Christians are confused about their liberty to gain material means. "The Christian should have nothing of this world's goods!" is an exclamation made by many a well-intentioned pilgrim. I believe that this does not represent the desire of God for his own. Dr. Baker James Cauthen was asked by a newly-appointed missionary about how much material they could take to the mission field with them. His reply was, "as much as you can take in your hands." His implication was that, when material goods begin to seize the heart they become too much. I would make the same observation to you. God is willing for you to have as much of this world's goods as you can hold in your hands without getting them in your heart. I will put it in other words . . . *God is willing to allow you to have as much as you will determine to use to glorify his name and extend his kingdom.* You can tell you have too much when it begins to lodge in your heart.

It is obvious that our adequacy is vital to the extension of the work of God. We cannot be a help to others while our needs are unmet. *The Amplified Version* says at this point, "So that you may always and in all circumstances and whatever the need, possessing enough to require no aid or support." I believe that this is a proper representation. God's will is our adequacy. But our adequacy is never an end in itself. We are made adequate that, through the means of our adequacy, the needs of others be met! This is the whole impact of the cycle. It does not end with us. We are merely a point along the circle of glory which begins with God and ends with God. We are vital to the continuity of the divine cycle because, through our sufficiency, are the needs of others met.

Now, having brought your circle down to the six o'clock position, label that point *You and I.* As we have designated in the illustration a space for your own needs, think of your many needs. God promises that we will be sufficiently supplied in all things pertaining to us. Now you have a half circle. You will observe the beginning point of God's ability and follow the circle of "abounding grace" down towards you and me. But that is only the beginning of the cycle. You and I are not the end of it, we are the *means* of it.

EVERY GOOD WORK IS THE MINISTRY OF IT.

Yes, the circle is only half complete! It has moved from God's ability at the top, along a line of abounding grace to you and me at the bottom. Now, move the circle on around counter-clockwise toward the top with the words around the circumference "that you may abound to every good work." Label the point at the three o'clock position "every good work." You may want to list within that circle every good work that you can think of. The church, mission causes outside the church, demands upon your time from worthy causes, special institutions established for the ongoing of the kingdom of God, needy individuals, and others *ad infinitum* could be listed here.

Notice the *quantity* mentioned here. It is "every" good work. This is a bold designation. There are hundreds and thousands of works across the world claiming to be good works. Almost every day mail crosses my desk from a cause claiming to be a good work. I am going to list in a moment several characteristics of a good work. When we have decided that a work is one which can be properly identified as a "good work" spiritually, we have settled the issue as to its support. God promises that as we abound with all grace, so we shall abound to every good work. As sufficient as God's grace has proved to be toward us, so will we prove sufficient to good works.

We now come to the *quality* of good works. What is a good work? Here are some guidelines for evaluating a work which claims to be a good work:

1. *It must have been initiated by the Lord.* God best anoints, confirms, and consummates what he has initiated. He is hesitant indeed to bless with divine glory that which was begun with human hands.

2. *It must be redemptive in nature.* God never supports a cause which does not fit properly into his overall plan of redemption. If it is not redemptive in quality, it doesn't deserve divine endowments.

3. *It must exist to God's glory, not man's.* If those involved in the plan have something to gain thereby, except the glory of God, that work may not be a good work. God will not share his glory with another—neither his praise with graven images.

4. *It must have as its purpose to exalt Jesus Christ in everything.* That which God is eager to bless is the platform upon which Christ will be exalted and from which Christ will be preached.

God is committed to every good work, but it must be understood that every work which claims to be good cannot go through all these gates. They might walk through one or two, or even three, but that is not enough. Ask these four questions of any work: *Did God initiate it? Is it redemptive? Does it exist for God's glory? Does it exalt Jesus?* If you can readily answer "yes" to all questions, then you may be assured that it is a good work indeed!

Isn't it good to know that there is ample support for any cause which will glorify God. I shall never forget the moment I began to suspicion this. It was long before I learned to think big according to his riches! I was still thinking small according to my poverty. I had just visited a dear widow lady regarding a gift her late husband had promised to make to the church. I was actually so scared of offending her that I dared not mention what amount I thought she should give. Even after she asked, I hedged by suggesting that she give what she thought best. I am glad that I made no suggestion, for the amount she gave was more than twice as much as I would have suggested! When I left that palatial mansion on the hill, I felt a strange mixture of emotions . . . of gladness for the gift, but shame for my little faith. Though it was a good work, I had so little faith that I would not suggest how much she should give!

As I drove down the hill from this dear widow's home this word came to me—God has no reason (or right, for that matter) to withhold anything from his children, regardless of magnitude, which will bring glory to his name! I know God was speaking to my heart. Though there was no audible voice, it was a definite message to my heart. After that statement had burned itself indelibly on my heart, my thoughts seemed to suggest, "Now, stop asking for peanuts and start claiming great things!" Think of it—no work established by God for God's glory and carried on in God's way will lack God's support! Glory!

Every good work is the ministry of the cycle of sufficiency.

Now follow in your illustration as the sweep of God's sufficiency moves on up from man's adequacy to every good work. Now you have three-fourths of a circle. It has begun with God's ability at the top, has swept its abounding grace to man's adequacy at the six o'clock position, has included all things that pertain to our own needs, and has moved through the means of our adequacy to all good works. But this is not the end. But the cycle or circle is not completed. When within the context of abounding grace, our personal adequacy, the needs of every good work are met, the end result is mentioned as "thanksgiving to God." "Being enriched in every thing to all bountifulness, which causeth through us *thanksgiving to God*" (2 Cor. 9:11). In the very next verse you have these words, "For the administration of this service not only supplieth the want of the saints, but is abundant also by many *thanksgivings to God*" (2 Cor. 9:12). Thus, we can say with Scriptural support . . .

THANKSGIVING TO GOD IS THE MOTIVE OF IT.

The closing verse of 2 Corinthians 9 says: "Thanks be unto God for his unspeakable gift!" (v. 15). With this doxology this great chapter on giving is concluded. Now the cycle is completed! But it is completed to begin again. Now, observe your completed circle denoting the finished cycle. It has begun with God's ability and returns to God's glory. We glorify God for his glorious ability and supply.

Next, let me suggest this exercise for you. Look at your illustration. Put your finger at the top of the circle where we begin with *God's ability.* As you move your finger around the circle counter-clockwise, begin to quote the verse . . . "God is able to make all grace" (2 Cor. 9:8). Continue to move your finger downward to the six o'clock position saying, "Abound toward you." Spend enough time there to observe that your adequacy and mine is the will of God as the means of our being used as "meeters of needs." Leave the six o'clock position and move toward the three o'clock position declaring, "that we being sufficient in all things may abound to every good work." You may want to write by your illustration several good works, good causes about which you have been concerned. Hold over these works the promise of God. Every good work is within the ministry of this cycle of sufficiency. Now move your finger around the remainder of the circle to declare that all this is to the glory of God and his thanksgiving. Now you have completed the CYCLE OF SUFFICIENCY!

There are some final questions. Are you in that circle? Are you experiencing sufficiency as you receive and bringing sufficiency as you give? Are you in the blessed flow of God's sufficiency? You can move in today. As you continue to read this volume, you will discover how to move into God's plan of economy. You may want to take a few moments to observe again the stages of the cycle. It is beneficial to review at intervals!

8
HOW LITTLE BECOMES MUCH

Sometimes we tire of listening to the details of a plan, regardless of how exciting the plan seems to be. It is good to leave details every now and then and take a field trip into the realm where the plan is really working!

Let's revisit the little lad with the five loaves and two fishes in John 6. He seems to be an ideal example of God's plan of economy in action.

You may identify with whomever you desire in the story. You may wish to identify with the hungry crowd as the pains of spiritual hunger gnaw at your heart even this very moment. You may wish to identify with the disciples who are as mystified with the problem as are the people. You may want to put yourself in the shoes of Philip as he answers the Lord about how the crowd would be fed. You may feel more comfortable in the place of Andrew who brings the lad to Jesus. Probably the one whose place is most envied is that of the lad. He comes off the hero of a sort, and a rich little hero at that! You may desire to stand in the place of the Master who has vision into the limitless resources of God. But from wherever you stand, you will be able to see how your little can become much!

THE PROBLEM
I remind you again that every miracle began upon the platform of a *problem.* I dare you to find a miracle that did not begin

in a problem. If we could ever see that we would have an entirely different attitude toward our problems. Problems are those situations engineered of God to bring us face to face with our deficiencies so we might view His sufficiency as our only alternative. We will discuss this more fully later, when we talk of the necessity of need.

Let us observe the problem. No little problem this! Here are thousands of people, and it is dinnertime. It is a long way to the closest eating place. The crowd may have been just 5,000, or it could have been as high as 20,000 with women and children. But after you get past 5,000 what difference does the number make if there is *nothing* to eat?

The problem simply stated is this: *There is a demand for which there is no apparent supply.* This is no new or uncommon thing in human experience. We are coming upon such situations all the time. We lose our composure when our supply of *patience* is exceeded by the circumstances which demand our patience. We become frustrated when our *love* supply is surpassed by the trying circumstances and trying people who both need and deserve our love. We weaken when our schedules and demands overwhelm our *physical* capacities. And many are the times when our outgo exceeds our income, both in money and other commodities.

We should realize from our reading of the Bible that we should learn to love our problems. Every problem is an opportunity to trust the Lord and to watch him step into circumstances to reveal his glory.

So you have run out! Patience is gone, love has waned, fatigue has overwhelmed, circumstances have demanded more than you can pay, and you find yourself bankrupt in more ways than one. You are fresh out! There is a great multitude, and you cannot feed them. There is a need, and you cannot meet it. There is a demand, and you cannot supply it. You knew all along that it might come to this, and while you are not surprised, you are nonetheless distraught and discouraged. Your suspicions that it might come to this were little help in preparing you for this moment! You are without recourse or resource.

YOU HAVE A PROBLEM. Good! This is the place to start a miracle. This is precisely where God chooses to begin the demonstration of the means of invading our *little* with his *much*.

THE PROBE

Once the *problem* has been acknowledged, the *possibilities* can be addressed. A part of the demonstration in this miracle centers around the approach of Jesus to the problem. He asked one of his typical disciples about the prognosis of the problem. The report was not encouraging. The situation was grave. The demand outweighed the supply. What Philip is really saying is, "Lord, it's an impossible situation!" He introduced a possibility so remote that it was out of the realm of reason. He said to the Lord, "two hundred pennyworth of bread is not sufficient." They certainly did not have that much!

It is interesting that Jesus asked the question to prove or to test Philip. Jesus knew what was in Philip. The outcome of his question was known before he asked it. Perhaps the reason he asked it was to demonstrate man's point of view as opposed to God's point of view. Philip would represent the former. Jesus would represent the latter.

The probe enlarged until surely all the disciples were scrambling for possibilities. How much like us they were! We are ever looking over the scene for human possibilities seeking to solve the problem with our own resources. Andrew comes with a lad. Perhaps he has sought out the lad or maybe the lad has sought him. But here they are, Andrew and the lad, one mystified, the other petrified. But it is at least a start. Philip didn't even offer this much.

THE PROSPECTS

Certainly, we would have to admit that the prospects were slim, but God always starts with slim prospects on the human side. It is a little insignificant seed that is sown, but manifold are the results. This seems to be a picture of God's way of doing things. That little lad and his lunch comprise the seed to be sown. It isn't much to start with, but praise the Lord, we don't have to stop where we started. In God's economy the seed is important. Our faith is the sowing of the seed to expect a miraculous harvest.

It is this kind of faith that brings a lad to Jesus and begins that process which releases the limitless resources of God. Though Andrew had a hesitant, retreating faith, it was enough to get the economy of God in motion. The faith was small but well-placed! A little faith in the right place and right person does more than much faith in the wrong place and the wrong person.

So there was an ever-so-small exchange between the lad and the Lord. No one there that day would have mistaken it for a business deal of any magnitude at all. But the fact was: that exchange tapped the eternal resources of heaven, and moved them into the bankrupt affairs of men, and met the need. That lad became so famous that, though no one knew his name, millions can identify him if you simply ask about the "lad and the loaves." The lad sowed a seed and stayed around to expect a miracle.

THE PROPOSITION

Now let us observe Jesus in action. He was the object of the giving of the little lad. He who had been the object of giving now would become the subject of giving. He Himself would give. This is a vital fact in making our little much. We must never break the giving cycle. Look at the proposition:

Jesus knew what he would do. He had already looked over into that other world of unseen, eternal reality and had the report of faith. He saw enough bread and fishes to feed the world.

He gave thanks. You can be sure that he gave thanks, not only for what his physical eyes saw, but what his spiritual eyes saw. His physical eyes saw the mighty problem and the minimum supply. His spiritual vision opened up the vastness of God's ability. "Adequate!" was the report of faith. The amount needed was beside the point! The complete adequacy of God was the entire issue.

Jesus' proposition is essentially the same with us today in the midst of our need . . . "I am in charge. I know what I am doing. Do as I say, and I will take care of the matter!"

And when he gave thanks there came the release of God's adequacy in the midst of man's inadequacy. The secret of this is the secret of life!

THE PROGRAM

I want you to notice several things about the program of feeding the multitude.

First, *I want you to see the thoroughness of the plans.* The plans would include the lad, his lunch, the disciples, the crowd, and the surplus when it was over. Jesus never misses a detail. There are times when we are prepared for anything but overwhelming success. I wonder sometimes if the Lord did bless our human machinery with abundant spiritual success if we would be prepared to take care of it. Jesus assumed success and was ready for the results. His plans were thorough.

Second, *observe the investment of the disciples.* Did they know what they were doing? Did they understand why they were doing what they were doing? Could they see the end of the action in which they were engaged? I think not! It involved faith to sow a seed. I suppose Jesus could have done it all himself, but this is not the way he did things. When he turned the water into wine, human instrumentality was used. The water may have turned into wine the very moment there was obedient faith on the part of those who carried the product to the governor of the feast. Our involvement is needed to fulfill God's intentions in his plan of economy.

Third, *observe the obedience of the multitude.* When the disciples came around with requests that the crowd be divided into groups of fifty and be made to sit upon the ground, there evidently was no protest. They simply did it!

Finally, *behold the secret which broke the miracle open* . . . GIVING! Jesus GAVE to the disciples. The disciples GAVE to the multitude. The GIVINGNESS of the lad continued with the GIVINGNESS of Jesus, which was passed on by the GIVING-NESS of the disciples. There was a contagion of giving! And the more that was given, the more there was to give. When giving took place, God moved within the affairs of men and released his resources! He will always do it!

That little lad did not have much to give. That is never the point. The point is that what he did give was enough to move the mightiness of God into the scene and demonstrate how man's little becomes God's much under the right conditions. When we learn to duplicate those conditions, God will do the same today.

THE PROOF

The proof of God's plenty was threefold.

First, *the people were filled.* They had enough. There was not one hunger pain that was not satisfied. Most of us would have stopped there. Our orientation generally stops with getting our needs met. Not so with Jesus. If it is great to *get* a blessing, then it is double great to *be* a blessing. I believe that this is where the surplus comes in.

Second, *there was enough left over for ministry.* There were twelve basketsful of food left over. There is the concept of ABOUNDING again. He who had given (the little lad) would now have the privilege of giving again. He had gotten in on the cycle and would never be the same again!

Third, *man's idea of Jesus was elevated.* They said, "This is of a truth that prophet that should come into the world" (John 6:14). Though their observation was incomplete, they began to recognize him to be more than a common man. They would have sought to force him to be their king, had he not dismissed himself to the mountain regions. Through this demonstration of the power of God, they knew that one more-than-a-man had been in their midst.

CONCLUSION

Now, let us observe the process that takes place as our little becomes much.

There is, first, the PROBLEM which creates DEMAND.

There is, second, the PROBE which reveals DOORWAYS.

There are, third, PROSPECTS that suggest DEPENDENCE.

There is, fourth, PROPOSITION which implies DEITY.

There is, fifth, a PROGRAM which brings DEMON-STRATION.

There is, sixth, a PROOF which supplies the DEMAND.

This story is repeated dozens of times in the Bible as man met mammoth problems with his little to discover that all of God's much was available to him.

9
THE CHURCH OF CENTURY TWENTY AND THE PLAN

The church of century twenty, as the saint, discovers some pressing paradoxes between what seems to be good business and faith. The Bible is silent on many issues that have become vital to our economy in this century. The church is a big business and must pay attention to some semblance of economic propriety. It cannot break all the rules of wise and sound economy and hope to get by. More churches have gone bankrupt within the past few years than I personally have heard about within all the years of my life. Some have gone bankrupt because of dishonesty somewhere. I trust that these are in the decided minority, and further that the dishonesty was outside the fold of the church. Others have come upon hard times because of a preoccupation with some areas which caused neglect in other areas. I cannot help but believe that most of these tragedies could have been avoided with the practice of wise and Scriptural economy.

But what is Scriptural economy? What does the Bible have to say about planning a budget, taking special offerings, launching into publicity programs of vast magnitude, or building a building? The Bible is, for the most part, silent regarding these matters. And yet, these are matters with which we must reckon. I conclude, therefore, that there is within the content and philosophy of the Scriptures the basis upon which we may build for the church a sound economy which can stand all the storms of earthly economy. This must certainly be expected within the context of claims already that there is a plan of economy, eternal in nature, which is so sound that nothing can destroy it and will be standing a million years from this moment. That plan, if universal and all-encompassing as we have claimed, surely includes the church as well as the individual.

THE POINT OF REFERENCE

While the written Word of God is the authority of truth, the local church is one of the expressions of the integrity of that truth. We can afford to be pragmatic with the Word of God. Being true, it works! And where it has not expressly outlined in detail the course of actions to be taken in a certain endeavor, its undergirding philosophy will guide us through any sea of economic uncertainty.

The point of reference as far as this chapter is concerned is both the Word of God and a local church: The Castle Hills Baptist Church in San Antonio, Texas, where I pastored for more than sixteen-and-one-half years. In this church I saw biblical concepts in the area of economy proved over and over again, both in the growth of the church as an institution and, more importantly, in the growth of the spiritual life of its membership. As far as I can detect, I plan to say nothing in this chapter that cannot be supported within the context of the work of God through this church.

I watched this church grow from a membership of slightly over 100 members to a membership of approximately 4,000. The total income for the year of our beginning was approximately $15,000. The total income for the last year I pastored the church was more than $700,000.

During that time we were in a major building program every three years. We used every conceivable method of financing the church buildings. We began the first program by selling church bonds. We then later arranged to borrow money from a local bank. Our latest building program involved raising the money over a brief period of time to virtually pay cash for a building.

This building cost more than $500,000 and was paid off shortly after it was occupied.

The church today possesses a thrilling spirit of giving among its members. It has a solid and balanced missionary budget and is a church known to care amply for its staff.

With this as a background, I want to speak about several items or areas which may fall into the class of things you have always wanted to know, but didn't know where to ask. Some statements will be the voicing of deep and deepening convictions, while others will evidence simply my own stated opinion. I shall try to distinguish between the two within the context.

THE CHURCH BUDGET

Though it would be difficult to justify a church budget in the Scriptures, the budget is well within the lines of biblical demands for decency and order. The Holy Spirit has an affinity for trained minds and orderly methods geared to his moving. A proper understanding of the church budget within the context of God's plan of economy is a most liberating feature in any church. There are some simple rules which I believe can be applied to the glory of God regarding the budget.

1. *The budget is a goal and not a god.* The budget is designed to be a tool, not a tyrant. It is created by people for the benefit of people to the glory of God. It is a goal and guide to that goal. It must not become an end in itself but must serve the end of economy in the local church.

2. *The budget should evidence faith in the future, and not bondage to the past.* Blessings of God must be anticipated, and that anticipation should be clearly reflected in the budget as a goal. Never did we adopt a budget with which we could have lived had not God come through with blessings and growth. We never set a budget we could obviously afford. Neither did you wait to get married until you could afford it.

The bride bent with age, leaned over her cane
Her steps uncertain need guiding . . .
While down the church aisle with a wan toothless smile,
The groom in a wheel chair gliding.

And who is this elderly couple thus wed?
You'll find when you've closely explored it,
That this is that rare, most conservative pair
Who WAITED 'TIL THEY COULD AFFORD IT!

A budget should be an evidence of the faith of the people in the limitless resources of God and his moving to make those resources available through his people.

3. *The budget should be the result of men and women having found the mind of God, and not the result of the conglomerate opinions of people.* It is still the church of the Lord Jesus Christ. He is still its Head. He is still in the business of sharing things with the church, and ours is the privilege of seeking his face until he speaks to us. If this is so, prayer must become more than a handy means of getting in and out of a committee meeting. Rule out the philosophy, "Let's pray first, so we can get down to business!" Prayer *is the business,* and budget committees, along with all others, should meet several times for nothing but prayer until they can get in the stream of God's thinking.

4. *The budget should be presented to involve as much of the church membership in a sense of responsibility as possible.* The broad base of responsibility in planning the budget will be of great help in presenting the budget. The more people that are involved in the comprising of the budget, the more excitement and approval there will be upon its presentation.

5. *The budget and finances of the church should be as much an item of prayer as missionaries and souls.* After all, if there is a breakdown in these areas, world evangelism will be greatly hampered. Thus, to pray for the finances of the church is to pray indirectly for every area of its worldwide responsibility.

It is no stronger than its weakest point!

ESTABLISHING A GIVING SPIRIT

A church develops a personality just like an individual does. A person can develop a greedy personality. Actually all he must do for this to happen is simply not give! A church can certainly adopt a disposition of "ungivingness" as well. I believe that several things are necessary in the establishing of a giving spirit on the part of the people in the church.

1. *Giving must be given its proper perspective as having God as its object.* Folks are not giving to the church alone. They are giving to God! David knew that the offering would go to the building of the Temple but he said, "All things come of thee, and of thine have we given thee" (1 Chron. 29:14).

2. *Giving must be given its intended purpose as involving man in the doings of God.* If we feature God as poor and about to go under if we do not give, we will develop a pitiful attitude toward God and a more pitiful one toward the church. All this worsens because of an even poorer attitude toward our money and ourselves.

3. *Giving must be presented as an endeavor of pleasure and not pressure.* We have already spoken of God's love for a cheerful giver. I am afraid that of all the givers I have known, only a small minority have achieved cheerfulness in giving! Contrast these two approaches to giving:

Approach One:
"Now, folks we have a need and we need to give to meet that need. If everyone will make a sacrificial gift, we will get out of this problem. If not . . . well, I don't know what will happen. We just must! Now let's all pitch in and do our part!"

Approach Two:
"Folks, there has come to us an opportunity! That opportu-

nity has come in the form of a need. We all know that a need is just a word from God that invites us to discover his supply! The opportunity to make this offering is an opportunity to get in on what God is up to! I want in on it—how about you? Ask what the Lord would have you do and know that what he commands he also enables. Praise the Lord for this opportunity!"

Which of these two approaches do you believe to be more appealing? Which of these approaches do you believe will result in the most enjoyable and spiritual offering? The answer should be easy!

4. *Giving must be an expression of response to needs of others, as well as to our love for the Lord.* The church should not shrink back from offerings necessitated by the needs of its members and others who are worthy of help. As I look back on the past years, some of the most vital times in our fellowship were when we responded to an immediate, unforeseeable need with the spontaneity of concerned hearts. No one is ever hurt, and everyone is always helped! He has promised to make us sufficient to *every* good work!

5. *The attitude toward giving on every level (money, time, self, etc.) must be developed with openness and boldness, and not fear and apology.* The worst catastrophe in this vein is that of someone's trying to take an offering in an apologetic and retreating manner. A legitimate need deserves a bold and enthusiastic approach! We can be sure that what Jesus said in Luke 6:38 is as applicable to the church as it is to the individual. "Give and it shall be given unto you!" I sought to teach my people that, invididually and corporately, there was no way to outgive God. I also added, "But it sure is fun to try!"

THE CHURCH AND THE TITHE

You will note in this whole volume an obvious lack of discussion regarding the tithe. This discussion will be brief. The tithe for

most is simply the gateway to the adventure of giving. We have
said that as a starting place it is good: as a stopping place it
is bad. The promotion of the tithe as a norm of giving is needless
and superfluous in a church where God's plan of economy has
been discovered. Folks who don't tithe are simply robbing God,
and there is no way around it! This should be made clear from
the pulpit. It is possible also to rob God in the area of the
offerings. The tithe, at best, seems to be a declaration which
says:

> "I recognize God as the Owner of all that is, and thus of
> all I have. As an indication of this, I will give from my
> first income one tenth of all I make. I will then seek the
> guidance of the Spirit in my offerings from then on."

If, all of a sudden, all of the tithe money which has been
withheld from God across the years were offered up to him and
the church, every church building in the world would be paid
off, every educational and missionary institution would be liberated financially, and billions of dollars would be made available
for the manning of the mission fields of the world.

The tithe is a place to begin to get in on God's plan of
economy.

BUILDING A BUILDING

I am about to state an opinion. A blessed and God-approved
opinion, in my estimation, but an opinion nonetheless. While
there are many ways to finance a building program, there is
a best way. God may bless many others (and obviously has!) but
there is one way that pleases him the most. This is the good
old-fashioned cash method! You say, "Impossible!" I say, "Right!"
And that is precisely where God can get into the situation with
you. Now, I have stated an opinion as to what is the best method.
I would urge anyone to exhaust every possibility of doing it this
way before resorting to another method.

I want to share with you the route the Lord caused me to take in coming to this conclusion. I began to see that there were about three very obvious things about borrowing money from a bank that were bothersome to me. These are:

1. When we get a loan from an institution, we are taking tithe and offering money and putting it back into the world. The interest we pay on that loan is not going back into God's cause. Of that you can be almost completely certain.

2. When we have paid back the loan thus borrowed, we will have virtually paid for the building twice, once in principle, and again in interest.

3. Most significantly, when we obtain a loan, we remove the possibility of the believers in the church participating in an endeavor in which they would have the privilege of believing God for a financial miracle in their lives.

On the basis of this, a challenge was presented to our people which was accepted. The result was briefly alluded to in the first part of this chapter. We went to the people for the total sum needed to build and furnish the building. The results were marvelous and memorable. A primary goal of $300,000 was surpassed by more than $200,000 with the entire $500,000 paid by the time we had been in the building less than one year! Out of that came many marvelous breakthroughs in the area of finances and faith. Our own family points back to this time as a corner-turning in our capacity to believe God in the matter of trusting in his resources.

There are two memorable precedents in the Old Testament that offer us much help in the structuring of offerings for major building campaigns. One is the case of Moses and the building of the tabernacle, and the other is that of David raising the support of the Temple. Both these endeavors could be entered in the books as "major." It is conservatively estimated that the tabernacle would cost in today's construction world approximately $10,000,000! The Temple would cost many times this if built today, possibly into the billions of dollars! And yet the method used to finance both these structures was the cash method! Now, I will admit that this was before the wonderful (or questionable) institution of credit was established!

I want to take the former of these two phenomenal endeavors and give an outline that I believe will be of help to you as you consider the direction your church should go. This wonderful story is recorded in Exodus 35 and 36. It is a most exciting story, and there are some statements that will take you literally right out of this world! I want to make five statements regarding the raising of the amount needed for the tabernacle with the hint beforehand that the same things should be true of any program or campaign that you should plan to carry out.

First, *the need for the program was God-caused.* It was nothing but the leadership, will, and desire of God in behalf of his people that presented the need for the tabernacle. He, who led his people out of slavery, gave them title right to the promised land, and miraculously opened up the Red Sea, now desired to have a meeting place where he could meet with his people. Thus, the need for the tabernacle—the tent of dwelling which would be both a symbol of the presence of God in their midst and the place where man could meet God. The tabernacle, priesthood, offerings, and system of worship were to present a glorious pre-view and preparation for the coming of the Lamb of God, who would take away the sin of the world. The tabernacle had to be to the last detail exactly what God commanded. Thus, the program was an outcome of a God-caused problem!

Likewise, the church of today needs to know that the problem which demands a new building, expansion of old buildings, or the relocation of facilities is a problem which God brought about. These are the kinds of problems I don't mind living with and responding to! If God's blessings brought these problems into existence, God's *further* blessings are sufficient to meet the needs the *former* blessings caused. God-caused problems certainly have God's unlimited resources for their solution!

Second, *the giving potential of the people was God-arranged.*

This is a beautiful case of *providence* with *foreknowledge*. God knew long beforehand that they would have the need for the tabernacle. Thus, before they left Egypt, he told Moses, "Speak now in the ears of the people, and let every man borrow of his neighbour [the Egyptians], and every woman of her neighbour, jewels of silver, and jewels of gold. And the Lord gave the people favour in the sight of the Egyptians" (Ex. 11:2-3). In the next chapter this fact is given in addition, "And the children of Israel did according to the word of Moses . . . And the Lord gave the people favour . . . so that they lent unto them such things as they required. And they spoiled the Egyptians" (Ex. 12:35-36). God looked into the future and provided in advance for what he would later require! He knows the need! He is never caught off guard!

Just as the potential was God-arranged in Moses' day, so does God know the potential of the people today. It cannot be computed by a system of analysis or by a human survey. Such surveys only serve to indicate what man could do if man did *his* best. But God is not impressed with what we can do by the doing of our best. He is eager to have us tap the resources that are reserved for those who are ready for God's best! Such resources in their availability are God-arranged.

Third, *the offering was God-directed*. They carried out the details of the offering according to the exact commandments of the Lord! Look at the specifications of the God-directed offerings.

1. It was to be a *freewill* offering. Ex. 35:5—"Whosoever is of a *willing* heart"; Ex. 35:21—" . . . every one whose heart stirred him up, and every one whom his spirit made *willing*"; Ex. 35:22—". . . as many as were *willing* hearted"; Ex. 35:29— "The children of Israel brought a *willing* offering."

2. It was a *revelation* offering. God was to command them what to give. Exodus 35:10—"And every wise hearted among you shall come, and make all that the Lord hath commanded."

3. It was to be an offering *Godward*. This is a vital point to

be regarded in all giving. We have mentioned this in an earlier chapter and will mention it again. GOD IS THE OBJECT OF ALL OUR GIVING. Ministries and churches may form a secondary object for our giving, but we must always give *to God.* Notice the references made which point to the Lord as the object of their offerings: Exodus 35:5—". . . an offering *unto the Lord*"; Exodus 35:21—"and they brought the *Lord's offering*"; Exodus 35:22—". . . an offering of gold *unto the Lord*"; Exodus 35:29— ". . . a willing offering *unto the Lord.*"

4. It was to be a *possible* offering. This is a picture of perfect providence. God required nothing of them that was beyond the reaches of his prearrangements! This is a thrilling note not to be found in many financial campaigns today . . . What God leads us to give, he has already prearranged! Isn't that a thrilling note! What God expects, God enables!

5. It was to be an *inclusive* offering. Such an endeavor as this includes everyone. Exodus 35:4—"And Moses spake unto all the congregation"; Exodus 35:22—"And they came, both men and women."

We may be perfectly certain that an endeavor which has been God-directed will not lack for God's power and prearranged resources!

Fourth, *the giving was God-inspired.* They gave *spontaneously.* The Lord seized their hearts, and their gifts were results of that blessed seizure! They gave *continuously.* The Lord moved in their hearts as they lay in their tents at night, and when the morning came, they showed up with more offerings. They gave *sufficiently.* It always works out that way. When God moves, there is a sufficiency. They gave a *surplus.* The report was given to Moses, "The people bring much more than enough!" (Ex. 36:5). Doesn't that have a good ring to it? MUCH MORE THAN ENOUGH! There was such a surplus that Moses had to issue a commandment for the people to stop giving! Oh, that this might happen somewhere in Christendom today! Listen to the record: "So the people were restrained from bringing. For the stuff they had was sufficient for all the work to make it, *and too much*" (Ex. 36:6-7).

Now, that is what I call a successful building program. That is God-inspired giving!

Fifth, *the results were God-glorifying*. Can you imagine the joy that filled their souls when the tabernacle was completed as they were able to say, "This is what God has done through us!" Look at the results:

1. God had a *house*. Now God could dwell in the midst of his people and meet them through the priest, revealing his nature through the system of offerings.

2. God's people had a *hope*. Every day that they saw the cloud and every night that they saw the pillar of fire, they were reminded that the God of heaven was leading them. This was their hope!

3. We have a *history*. In 1 Corinthians 10:11 we read, "Now all these things happened unto them for ensamples: and they are written down for our admonition upon whom the ends of the world are come." This inspiring account has moved many a congregation to launch out on God and do things God's way, only to discover that the *God who lived in Moses' day is just the same today!* Praise the Lord!

> Look at the facts again:
> THE NEED WAS GOD-CAUSED.
> THE POTENTIAL WAS GOD-ARRANGED.
> THE OFFERING WAS GOD-LED.
> THE GIVING WAS GOD-INSPIRED.
> THE RESULTS WERE GOD-GLORIFYING.

I can recommend to you these guidelines and safely guarantee satisfaction to all in your next building program.

THE OFFERING AS WORSHIP

In most churches where I have worshiped, the time of the offering is a great wasteland. It is a time mixed with an uncertain combination of toleration, people-looking, music-listening, or news-whispering. It would certainly be far-fetched to label it worship! I believe, however, that it can and should be a time of exciting worship. Let me make some suggestions:

First, introduce the time of offering as a vital part of the service. The pastor might say, "Now we come to a part of the service that is vital both to God and to us. It is time for the offering. God has chosen in his sovereignty to allow us to have a part in his kingdom enterprises. I invite you to pray regarding your response to this God-given opportunity. Do not treat this moment lightly. The consequences will be eternal."

Second, urge everyone to have a part in the offering. It sometimes helps to remind them that Jesus was visiting the place of worship and (of all places) sat over against the treasury. He watched the people as they gave, but the one who gained his attention was a widow who put in a small amount. He immortalized that unnamed widow when he stated that she had given more than them all! The pastor might suggest, "The same Savior who sat over against the treasury is here today and knows the amount, the spirit, and the love of your gift. If you have no relationship with the risen Lord, wait to make your gift and make your relationship right with him now! If you have grudges or resentments or others have aught against you, leave your gift and be reconciled, and then come back. The Savior is waiting and watching for your response."

Third, you might desire to use a ritual of giving. I have found this especially delightful! On the occasion of the great offering that was taken by David for the building of the Temple, there was great joy. "And the people rejoiced for they offered willingly . . . and David the king also rejoiced with great joy" (1 Chron. 29:9). Then there followed what I call an offertory doxology. Listen to it:

"Thine, O Lord, is the greatness, and the power, and the glory, and the victory, and the majesty:
for all that is in the heaven and in the earth is thine;

thine is the kingdom, O Lord, and thou art exalted as head above all.

Both riches and honour come of thee, and thou reignest over all;

and in thine hand is power and might;

and in thine hand it is to make great, and to give strength unto all.

Now therefore, our God, we thank thee, and praise thy glorious name.

But who am I, and what is my people, that we should be able to offer so willingly after this sort?

for all things come of thee, and of thine own have we given thee" (1 Chron. 29:10-14).

That is a glorious doxology to present at the outset of the offering period. It is helpful for the people to follow the pastor in saying this out loud in unison. It is a word of praise, and God inhabits the praise of his people!

Fourth, one key to a meaningful and worshipful offering period is that of variation. The Doxology would be one variation. Waiting for a prayer—at the close of the offering—asking the Lord to bless the gifts given, as those gifts are held up to the Lord, would be another approach. A two-minute exhortation regarding the privilege of giving from the pastor or a selected layman would be helpful. I challenge you to creativity regarding this terrific opportunity in your church.

I have discovered without variation (as far as I can now remember) that any church where God has moved to liberate in the area of giving has also been liberated in other areas of economy as well. That church seems not to lack for love, excitement, concern, workers, or resources to do the task assigned by the Lord.

I pray that your church will become a supernatural church in that you discover together the limitless resources available to those who make their resources available to God and launch out on him.

10
OPENING THE WINDOWS OF HEAVEN

"And prove me now herewith, saith the Lord of hosts, if I will
not open you the windows of heaven, and pour you out a blessing,
that there shall not be room enough to receive it" (Mal. 3:10).

God's plan is not only the source of the best way of life for
man on earth but also its neglect is the basis of divine judgment.
If accepted, it liberates; if rejected, it brings bondage. All people
everywhere are in bondage or freedom depending on their response to the plan of God.

The people of God in Malachi's day had departed from God's
ordinances, doubted the value of serving him, and distrusted his
ability to care for them. But as always, it is God who takes the
initiative in getting man on the right track. It is the offended
(God) seeking out the offender (man) and wooing him back to
obedience. These verses in the third chapter of Malachi chronicle
one of those many times when the God of heaven, whose holiness
has been violated by man's carelessness, courts rebellious man
and makes the way back to Him clear. These verses become
a guide for men and women in every age to discover the way
back to God. If they needed to know in Malachi's day how to
open the windows of heaven, how much more in our day do
we need the secret of opening those windows. This is precisely
where God's plan of economy comes in. It was at the point of
God's economy where the violation had occurred. It was precisely
at this point that there must be return.

THE POINT OF RETURN
When God's plan is rejected, all that God would do for his

106

people is disallowed. Judgment is the only alternative. The disposition of God, however, is always this, "Return unto me, and
I will return unto you" (Mal. 3:7). But what is the point of return?
This is a question which must be answered in the life of the
nation, as well as in the life of the individual, if we are to get
back to God's way of doing things. Here is a rule which we
do well to keep in mind: THE POINT OF RETURN IS ALWAYS
THE POINT OF DEPARTURE. Wherever we have departed
from the doing of God's will is the point where we must begin
our return. God says, "Will a man rob God? Yet, ye have robbed
me." When they asked, "Wherein have we robbed thee?" the
answer came back quickly, "In tithes and offerings" (Mal. 3:8).
It was as simple as that. The tithe was a basic admission that
God was the source of everything, and this requirement was his
right. It was to be paid as an indication that it all belonged
to God and as a recognition of the place of priority God held
in their lives. Thus, as long as this area was unattended, there
could be no relationship between the offenders and God. They
might have returned in some other point putting away their idols.
They might have resumed their regular worship. They might
have doubled their time spent in prayer. But until the point
of departure which was in their giving (or lack of it) became
the point of return, there could be no revival.

As strange as it seems, our finances generally mark the position
of our spiritual pilgrimage. We are no further along in our overall
walk with God than we have learned to trust him in our material
prosperity. When we have departed at this point, we cannot
compensate in other areas and get by. This becomes the point
of return. If you, dear reader, are not right in the area of finances
and material things, your economy is off balance . . . the whole
of your economy. Finances comprise an index for the entire
spectrum of economy. Things will not get any better until we
tend to this area. This one area can be the reason for unresolved
conflicts, unmet needs, and broken fellowship.

I have read more information in national news on the economy than ever I can remember. It seems to me that more than one half of the total information in most of the news magazines has to do with the economy. Yet, in the thousands of words I have read, I have not heard among the suggestions for survival one word of advice that we return to God's way. Yet, I can tell you without any doubt in my mind that there shall be no recovery of the economy without paying attention to the Word of God. We may take emergency measures, do some patchwork, adopt some superficial stop-gap methods, or seek to inject new life into our economy through more government aid, but there will not be recovery! It is at this point that we must return, or there will be no return.

PRONOUNCING OF RETRIBUTION

God simply said, "Ye are cursed with a curse: for ye have robbed me, even this whole nation" (Mal. 3:9). Have you ever thought of America under a curse? And if America is under a curse, there is a measure in which every one of its citizens abides under the conglomerate results of that curse. Look at the last years in the life of our nation. With all the suggestions of a New Deal, a New Frontier, The Great Society, we have a catastrophe. In two decades we have seen the stock in American integrity at home and abroad sink to an all-time low. We have been made to look like fools in two "no win" wars. The last one in Southeast Asia brought our prestige at home and around the world to an all-time nadir. And the price we paid for this was 56,000 choice human lives, not to speak of billions of dollars to finance defeat.

Have you ever thought that just as a nation can place itself under a curse by disregarding God's plan, so can an individual? Let these words fall with a dull thud on your heart: "Ye are cursed with a curse!"

Israel was a nation chosen as a vehicle for the truth of God and, therefore, was responsible for the stewardship of this trust. Now, the result was a curse upon the whole nation. Surely

America has been blessed of God with the opportunity to reach the world with the gospel of Christ. And yet the nation which has the capacity to gain a hearing on behalf of Christ throughout the whole world seems to be under a curse. In education, politics, religion, and even in natural resources there seems to rest a pall of gloom and doom. But alas, it need not be this way!

PROPOSITION FOR RECOVERY

The offended God makes the concession. If they would return to obedience at the point of their disobedience, God would answer. The tithe would be an indication of a changed heart toward God. It would be man's "amen" to the promise of God, his commitment to God's trustworthiness. When God gives a proposition to man and man does not heed it, the sin is manifold. It is a sin against the *person* of God. Refusal to respond is the fiercest accusation of the integrity of God. It is a sin against the *power* of God. God holds all things in his power, and his propositions are based upon his power. To refuse his advances is to stand against his power. It is a sin against the *promise* of God. If I make a promise to you that is good and advantageous to you and you reject it, that is not a neutral act, but an act of offense.

But here God opens the door to recovery, "Bring ye all the tithes into the storehouse . . . and prove me now herewith . . ."— here is a proposition to profit—". . . if I will not open you the windows of heaven" (Mal. 3:10). Who can tell all that this involves? Has there ever been a time when we so needed to know how to open the windows of heaven as today? Has there ever been an era in your own personal life when you so keenly felt the need of knowing how to tap heaven's resources as now? Here is the information! Respond to God's proposition with your material means. Let that be an indication that you believe that all you are and have belongs to Him. This is where we can start. What could "opening the windows of heaven" involve? I want to make several suggestions.

One, it surely suggests the acknowledgments of mutual responsibilities. Two, it inevitably declares resumption of communications between heaven and earth. Three, it must include the availability of heaven's resources for earth's needs. Getting the windows of heaven open should be a priority item in our world.

PROMISES FOR THOSE RETURNING

Now, remember that all these promises were contingent upon their returning to God's way of doing things in the material realm. Keep in mind that all the following blessings were promised merely upon their response in the area of their money!

"I will pour you out a blessing" (Mal. 3:10). There are two things obvious from these words. The quality of the blessings will be sudden. He would "pour out" a blessing. The result of obedience would be immediate. That fairly well sums up . . . *sudden* and *immediate!* But notice further the *quantity* of that blessing . . . "there shall not be room enough to receive it!" Imagine it, not room enough to receive it! That simply means that we shall have to give it away. This more-than-enough blessing of God belongs to all who will meet his conditions. That is a far cry from haunting need in so many areas where the cry is "not enough." This is the kind of economy that man's rebellion leads to . . . "not enough." God wills it that every child of his know the kind of economy where there is "not room enough to receive it." Let's look further at the specific nature of that blessing.

"I will rebuke the devourer for your sakes" (Mal. 3:11). Once we step back within the confines of God's economy, then there can come the supernatural protection of God. God will personally rebuke the devourer. If that devourer is a plague upon the crops, God's rebuke will destroy the plague. If that devourer is illness, then illness must flee or come under authority. If that devourer is recession or depression, then God will personally neutralize the results of such conditions. The promise to rebuke the devourer is a terrifically broad promise. I am convinced that it is as wide as the world and covers anything or anybody that comprises a threat to the well-being of the people of God.

"All nations shall call you blessed" (Mal. 3:12). It was the blessing of God upon the children of Israel which caused the harlot Rahab to come to faith in God. She said, "I know that the Lord hath given you the land, and that your terror is fallen upon us, and that all the inhabitants of the land faint because of you. For we have heard how the Lord dried up the water of the Red Sea" (Josh. 2:9-10). Here was a woman of the street who had not much spiritual aptitude, but who had clear enough vision to see that this group of people was especially blessed by the God of heaven. God said, "All nations shall call you blessed." It is one thing to call yourself blessed, but it is another for others to see such a measure of heaven's treasures that they call you blessed! When the signs of God's blessings are obvious, the hearts of the enemies of the Lord will melt.

Now, this is what I want you to see. We give to God not because he has nothing and is dependent upon our gifts. If we give from such a motive, we shall have a depreciated idea and concept of God. Man is to give to get in on God's program. IF YOU WILL GIVE, I WILL GIVE! This is the promise of God. Where is there mention of the puny gifts of man after God says, "I will open the windows of heaven!"? The significance of man's gifts in tithes and offerings is found in the fact that, when they are presented, there is a release of the vast treasures in the storehouse of heaven. The dynamic of our giving is that by this means God chooses to open the windows of heaven and get heaven's resources in on our needs. Our giving moves God into action! It always has, and it always will! Though this is an Old Testament promise, the principles remain the same! Praise the Lord! It is for you and me as individuals and is a proposition for the nations of the world. And God is still speaking. His disposition is the same! IF YOU WILL RETURN, I WILL RETURN!

11
THE PROMISE TO PROSPER

"But my God shall supply all your need according to his riches in glory in Christ Jesus" (Phil. 4:19).

DEFINING PROSPERITY

We have elsewhere defined *prosperity* as "that status in which one has all he needs and the capacity to enjoy it." We have extended that definition to include "the capacity to move God into action at the point of our needs." The one thing that I want you to notice about these definitions is that prosperity is all-inclusive. True prosperity covers every area and commodity in life. One is not prosperous in the true sense of the term when one is rich in money and poor in peace of mind, or rich in material matters while poor in emotional health. I cannot help but think that the promises of the Bible which pertain to riches and prosperity surely must include the whole of life. With true prosperity, the digits of one's bank account, vastness of real estate holdings, or number of bedrooms in one's residence are facts that have little bearing. We all have known people who were long on all these and yet short of the greatest treasure of them all . . . a sense of peace with God and one's inner self.

Peace and prosperity are mentioned together as qualities to be admired. "Pray for the *peace* of Jerusalem: they shall *prosper* that love thee. *Peace* be within thy walls and *prosperity* within thy palaces" (Ps. 122:6-7). Both terms seem to suggest a completed state. The doxology of God to his people before they came into the land of promise was this: "This book of the law shall not depart out of thy mouth; but thou shalt meditate therein day and night, that thou mayest observe to do according to all that is written therein: for then thou shalt make thy way prosperous, and then thou shalt have good success" (Josh. 1:8).

There is much talk about riches in the Bible. David affirmed in 1 Chronicles 29:12: "Riches and honour come of thee." The preacher in Proverbs 22:4 said, "By humility and fear of the Lord are riches, and honour, and life." The same preacher declared that there was a vital connection between trusting the Lord with our firstfruits and prosperity. He said, "Honour the Lord with thy substance, and with the first fruits of all thine increase: so shall thy barns be filled with plenty and thy presses shall burst with new wine" (Prov. 3:9-10).

Paul affirms that it is God's intention to make us rich. "For ye know the grace of our Lord Jesus Christ, that, though he was rich, yet for your sakes he became poor, that ye through his poverty might be rich" (2 Cor. 8:9). Obviously, the context demands a broader wealth than material things, but who would argue that it does not include those things?

For now we shall accept from our text what seems to be the best and briefest definition of prosperity: ALL NEED SUPPLIED! I doubt that we could find a better definition if we looked the world over!

Let us look at this great passage of Scripture for an examination of the richness of its promise. I can safely say that a miraculous transformation in life-style awaits anyone who simply believes this passage and lives out the terms of that belief. I want to examine the *direction* of the promise, the *dynamic* of the promise, the *dimension* of the promise, and the *disposition* of the promise.

THE DIRECTION OF THE PROMISE

Within the context of the whole passage, it becomes clear that Paul is talking to folks who have been in the practice of giving. He refers to their "communicating to his affliction" (Phil.

4:14). He states in verse fifteen that they (the Philippians) were the only ones among the churches who had communicated with him regarding giving and receiving. They had sent twice to his necessity while he was in Thessalonica. Thus, he is expressly talking with those who communicated with his need by giving, and giving again, to his needs. While the verse may be taken by many to be universal to everything on every level, its context demands that the safest ground is the qualification of a giving heart. As we are sensitive to the needs of others, it is God who sees to our supply. Here again is the principle that we encountered in Luke 6:38, "Give, and it shall be given unto you." Those who become the sources of meeting the needs of others will discover that God is the source of meeting theirs.

THE DYNAMIC OF THE PROMISE

With Paul, it was a direct declaration. There was no mincing of words. You can stand on what he said, and for that matter, there is room for all the world to stand. His confession is, "MY GOD SHALL." There are three great foundation stones upon which stands the dynamic of this promise.

One, there is the authenticity of Paul's experience. He was speaking from the platform of a life in which his own needs had been supplied. As he abandoned himself to the meeting of the needs of others, he discovered that God could meet all of his needs. He said in summary, "I have strength for anything through him who gives me power" (Phil. 4:13, NEB). Paul was not presenting theory but discovery. He had discovered that he did not have a need which had not been supplied by the perfect grace of God. He himself stood as a completed testimony of the claim that he had made. He knew that God could meet their needs because God had so completely met his.

Second, there was the inspiration of Paul's utterance. Had there been no experience to back it up, no provision on record, the fact would have been just as true. The Holy Spirit had breathed into Paul's heart this utterance of faith. He was speaking without fear in behalf of God. Ringing fresh in his memory was what he had heard God say when the removal of the thorn was sought, "My grace is sufficient for thee"—that declaration transformed Paul's pleading prayer into praise, and he said, "Most gladly therefore will I rather glory in my infirmity, that the power of Christ may rest upon me" (2 Cor. 12:9).

Third, there is the unchanging character of God. The whole Bible is an unimpeachable record of the ability of God to meet every need which can exist within his world. He has never been at a loss. Corrie ten Boom was right when she said, "There is no hand-wringing in heaven!" God is never in panic. There is no situation that is greater than his ability to care for. James presents him as the God "with whom there is no variableness, neither shadow of turning" (Jas. 1:17).

The power of the promise, "MY GOD SHALL," rests with the ability of God! (See Phil. 4:19). Those words are the proper answer to many questions which have been asked amid the distress of the world and many more which have not even been asked yet! MY GOD SHALL!!

THE DIMENSIONS OF THE PROMISE

I want to stand at a vantage point which looks out upon two directions . . . *from* the supply and *toward* the need. These two designations give us the dimensions of the promise, "My God shall supply" (Phil. 4:19).

When I was a child we used to play a game that was very frustrating to me at times. We would try to say a number that was greater than a number that already had been given. The one who could think of the greatest number was the winner. I would come up with a new plan and would be convinced that no one could outdo me when I said, "forty billion quadrillion!" Now, how could anybody think of a number bigger than that. But some wise guy would say, "ten times forty billion quadrillion!" And off we would go again into the infinity of numbers. God has, in much the same manner, stated an amount beyond which we cannot go. We can name the quantity of our needs and raise that quantity to a point beyond our imaginations, but the answer is satisfyingly the same: "My God shall supply all your need!" The measure is ALL! There is no maximum beyond which God's ability to provide cannot go. God is committed to *every* need!

The commitment to meet every need is backed by God's vast resources . . . "according to his riches in glory." Oh, if we could only get a view of those resources! We have already established the fact that God has all the wealth in this world and the next in his possession. The only means we have of measuring wealth is in terms of our economy. I have a feeling that when we receive a view of "his riches in glory" that we will gasp out a response like the Queen of Sheba when she saw Solomon's splendor . . . "The half was not told me" (1 Kings 10:7). There are all kinds of riches. The ones most fleeting are those our senses can register and appreciate. In the unseen realms are the real riches. One day we shall look through the obvious and see the actual. When we do, we are bound to know just a blast of regret that we lived so poorly and so punily when our actual prosperity was so plenteous.

Did you notice the words "according to"? It might have been "out of," but it wasn't! Had you ever thought of the significance of this designation? It is vital. The best way I know to illustrate the difference in "according to" and "out of" is in this parable. Two men serve on the Board of Trustees of one of our institutions. That institution is strapped with financial needs. The plea for financial help is made by the board president and the head of the institution. Both these board members are millionaires. Both of them respond by taking out a checkbook and writing a check to the institution. One writes a check for $1,000, and the other writes a check for $40,000! Now, while it can be rightly said that both men gave *out of* their resources, it can significantly be said that the latter gave *according to* his resources! Do you see the difference! (By the way, I recently ministered in a city where a wealthy man gave such a gift to a local college.)

I was chairman of the board of trustees of one of our vital missionary education institutions for more than ten years. During those days we practiced believing God for every need. We began in cramped quarters in a very rough section of the city and progressed to a multi-million-dollar facility on several acres of land adjacent to a major thoroughfare.

I remember in one vital board meeting, our discussions were centering on a need for dormitory space. We concluded that the cost at that time might be about $150,000. Sitting in that board meeting was a man who was a great Christian and whose gift was that of giving. He said nothing, and I do not remember that I expected him to say anything. After the board meeting I came back to my office, and almost immediately a call came for me. It was this board member and his to-the-point declaration was, "My wife and I have talked over this matter, and we want to make a gift that will enable us to build this dormitory!" I could not believe my ears. In fact, I made him say it again so I would be sure that I was not hearing things. And give that gift he did! He not only paid for the construction of the building, but for the furnishings as well, and past that, he has given again and again! That is a case of giving according to your riches. When that kind of giving takes place, the needs are not just barely met . . . they are absolutely met!

"My God shall supply all your need according to his riches." Nineteen wide centuries have come and gone, empires have crumbled, vast kingdoms of wealth have disappeared into antiquity, and God's ability to meet needs according to his riches in glory has not waned one whit! World economies have come and gone. Could we have stood in Caesar's day and viewed the greatness of his kingdom, we could not have imagined a day when that kingdom was no more! But it fell and went the way of all things of the earth. Paul was indeed right when he said, "The things which are seen are temporal" (2 Cor. 4:18). The palace of Caesar and the palaces of many who have followed

in his train are pulverized. The coffers of great empires have
long since been emptied. The glory of great dynasties is gone,
vanished. BUT GOD'S VAST SUPPLY OF RICHES OF EVERY
KIND HAS NOT BEEN DRAINED ONE IOTA! He still supplies
every need according to riches in glory! Evidently, glory is still
full! Praise the Lord!

THE DISPOSITION OF THE PROMISE

The last words of the promise are "by Christ Jesus." We are
not absolutely certain whether this is "by" or "in" since the
word in the Greek is the same for both. The ambiguity may
add to the blessing! *It may be either and could be both!* In the
one (in), Jesus is the *depository* of God's riches; in the other (by),
he is the *administrator* of God's riches. Our wealth is in him,
and he is in us the administrator of all that wealth! Let's look
at both possibilities.

"In Christ" is the *location* of all the riches of God. We are
told in Ephesians 1:3 that we have been blessed with all spiritual
blessing *in Christ* in heavenly places. We have the information
from Colossians 2:3 that all the treasures of wisdom and knowledge are hid *in Christ.* In both of these cases, the Greek *locative*
is used, denoting location. The little Greek word *en* can either
be translated *in* (locative) or *by* (instrumental) which denotes
"by the means of."

"By Christ" is the *administration* of all the riches of God.
For instance, in Colossians 1:16-17 we read that all things were
created *by* Christ and that *by* him all things are held together.
The same word *en* is used, but in the instrumental case. Now
this changes the meaning somewhat so as to say, "All things
came about by means of him, and all things are held together
by means of him." In yet another case in Ephesians 3:21 we
read, "Unto him be glory in the church by Christ Jesus throughout
all ages, world without end." The "by" again is designated by
the same word *en,* but is used in the instrumental case. It is
by the means of Christ that glory shall come to God.

So take your choice! If you translate it "in Christ Jesus," he is your *depository.* If you translate it "by Christ Jesus," he is your *administrator.* What a delightful dilemma to be forced to peruse these two choices. My conclusion is this: in the etymological realm, it could be either; in the practical realm of reality, it definitely is both! Our riches are *in* him, and our riches are *by* him.

Now, let us make a concluding overview of the passage again.

The *direction* of the promise is to those who had already responded to others' needs.

The *dynamic* of the promise was linked to the unlimited power of God and is backed by his limitless resources. "My God shall supply . . ."

The *dimensions* of the promise are "all need" and "according to his riches in glory."

The *disposition* of the promise is "by [or in] Christ Jesus." Jesus is the one who makes disposition of the riches of God. He is both the fountain's flow and the fountain's source.

Further consider this:

"My God" . . . how personal! Paul is saying, "He is the God in whom I have found this secret of contentment of which I have been telling you. God of my fathers? Yes! God and Father of our Lord Jesus Christ? Yes! But what I am now writing to you reflects the inconceivably intimate fact that he is my God."

"Will supply" . . . how *positive!* There is no quibbling, no small print in the promise. He simply will! He will fill up to the full!

"Every need of yours" . . . how *provident!* This is so vital that instead of dealing with this here, I am going to devote an entire chapter to the understanding of needs. That word *need* is absolutely vital to the working out of the terms of the economy.

"According to his riches in glory" . . . what *plentitude!*

Paul Rees said it well when he said, "The Father's infinite capacity for *giving* is his child's adequacy for *living.*"

"By [or in] Christ Jesus" . . . what *presence!* In whatever capacity we are viewing Christ at the moment, whether as source or means, the glorious fact is that both require his *presence* to make them valid! Thus, the pivotal truth is that while he has all riches deposited in himself and is the means by which all riches come to us, HE IS HIMSELF ALL WE NEED so that we may say of any situation or circumstance, "For this I have Jesus."

So there you have it! God's glorious plan of economy stated in another way. The testimony of Paul is of complete adequacy! We should use this verse as a gate each morning and evening and throughout the day. We need constant reminding of this truth. We need to get through the visible to the real, where God is operating to meet our needs all the time.

Fellow pilgrim, have you brought unmet needs to the end of this chapter? Are you in circumstances that could be easily labeled "not enough"? Have you had checks come back in your emotional account marked "insufficient funds"? I want you right now to make a confession that cuts through the apparent to the actual. I want you to lay aside what your accountant tells you, what the stock market tells you, what your emotions tell you, and listen to what God tells you! Quit confessing as true what seems to the senses to be true. Simply say aloud right now the words of our text, "My God shall supply all your [my] need according to his riches in glory by Christ Jesus." Say it again and again until you have memorized it. Tell God that you believe that verse 100 percent! Tell the devil that you refuse to believe anything contrary to that verse. Begin to praise God that the verse is true in every circumstance in which you now find yourself.

You are now ready for the next chapter. Meet a new friend . . . need! The presence of need has caused you to panic before! Count need a necessary friend which makes a demand upon the riches of God!

12
THE NECESSITY OF NEEDINESS

"My God shall supply all your *need*" (Phil. 4:19).

NEEDINESS: noun, The state of being in want; poverty. (Britannica World Language Dictionary)

I love to close the old year out in prayer and praise. I have tried to do this for many years. This particular year was no different, except that I was alone and nursing a cold. I thanked God for a wonderful year . . . the greatest ever in every way I could think of. I wondered what in the world the Lord could do for an encore. I could not imagine him revealing himself in any more a delightful manner than he had in the past year. I was sure that God wanted to do more to the glory of his name the coming year than he was able to the year before. But what could I do to cooperate with him? How could I react so as to be an instrument in his hand whereby he could do more? I knew that it was a possibility to try so hard doing things for God that I could get in his way and hinder him instead of helping him. I was moved to read the verse that comprised our text for the previous chapter. "My God shall supply all your need according to his riches in glory by Christ Jesus" (Phil. 4:19).

Now, I had read that verse many times before. I could quote it from memory. I had even preached on it more than one time, I am sure. But I read it again. I rehearsed its riches and received the promise from God for an unlimited grant for all the needs that I would ever have. Then, all of a sudden the word jumped off the page and into my heart, and I saw one word stand out above all the rest: N-E-E-D! That word became the hinge on which the whole verse swung. Then it hit me! Of course, this is the key! The more needs there are, the more God does, for God operates on the basis of need. If God is to do more, there must be more need. Need is the springboard of his doing! He only operates amid need.

I began to see a law . . . the law of supply and demand. There is sweet because there is bitter. There is heat because there is cold. There is light because there is darkness. The former in each case is of value because of the latter. There is good because there is evil. There is victory because there is defeat.

THERE IS SUPPLY BECAUSE THERE IS NEED.

Now, I must admit that I have never developed a love for neediness. I have had some experience in both abounding and being abased, and the former has my vote! I simply do not like to be in need. And yet that night as I pondered both future and past, the Lord seemed to be saying to me, "If I am to do more in your life to my glory, you must allow me to create needs in your life to which I can be the total supply. You will not trust me without need. If there are no problems or needs, then there will be no cause for you to be dependent on me as the supply in every situation. I will supply the total fulfillment to every need I allow!"

Though I was a little bit shocked at this revelation, I prayed, "Lord, then let the needs come!" Have you ever prayed a prayer that you sometimes almost wished you hadn't prayed? God took me seriously. He opened the gate to need. Friend, my life was filled with needs . . . all kinds of needs. Everything that wasn't nailed down began to come loose. I cried to the Lord, asking him what in the world he was doing to me. He merely reminded my heart that he was just answering my prayer! I tried to remind myself that I was supposed to be living the life of victory and was not supposed to have need. (This is a common misconception making the rounds today!) The months since then have been filled with more needs than any period in my life. I can report to you now that God has kept his Word. He has met every need according to his glory by Christ Jesus!

I began to see how wrong it is to reject neediness, since this is precisely what triggers the divine supply. The life of victory is lived right in the midst of need! It is our weakness in the warfare that calls God's power into the battle. It is the need that releases the supply! The church that Jesus was most severe with in the book of Revelation is quoted as saying, "I am rich, and increased with goods, and have need of nothing." The Lord of the Lampstands said in return, "Thou . . . knowest not that thou art wretched, and miserable, and poor, and blind, and naked" (Rev. 3:17).

Neediness is a necessity! We must have need. This is what calls God into our affairs. Let's get acquainted with neediness.

IDENTIFYING NEEDINESS

Need has many faces. There are many words used in the Bible to identify it. The psalmist used the word *distress*. He said, "Thou hast enlarged me when I was in distress" (Ps. 4:1). Again he said, "I called upon the Lord in distress: the Lord answered me, and set me in a large place" (Ps. 118:5).

Paul had many names for need. In 2 Corinthians 12:9-10, he gives us several synonyms for need. He calls it weakness, infirmities, reproaches, necessities, persecutions, and distresses. In Romans 5:3 he discusses tribulations, stating that we should glory in them.

James exhorts to "count it all joy when ye fall into divers temptations" (1:2). Such testings are absolutely necessary, he declares, to the maturity which equips us for anything.

In each of these three cases there are things mentioned that are repulsive to our minds. Who of us would choose distress over delight? Yet, we know that we can learn more of God and have more done for our integrity in a few hours of distress than in a month of delight. And the psalmist cited distress as the means through which comes enlargement (Ps. 4:1). Who would choose reproaches, weakness, and persecutions over against a life of ease? Yet Paul testified, "Most gladly therefore will I rather glory in my infirmities" (2 Cor. 12:9). And there is evidence that we are exhorted to rejoice in our present sufferings more than in our future splendor. Listen to what Paul says in Romans 5:2-3, "Let us exult in the hope of the divine splendour that is to be ours. More than this: let us even exult in our present sufferings, because we know that suffering trains us to endure, and endurance brings proof that we have stood the test" (NEB).

Thus, it is crystal clear that neediness is a necessary ingredient in God's plan of economy. If we are to be a part of God's glorious plan of economy, then we must get accustomed to neediness. It is upon the platform of our neediness that the fire of God's supply falls.

Do you have a need? Don't hide it, or deny it, or disregard it! Rejoice in it, for it is an opportunity to see God's supply. That is precisely the reason for it. Oh, if we could see this! How we scramble to stay out of need when God is obliged to put us in whatever need and distress it takes to move us into the realm of his wonderful supply. He loves us that much! He gives us needs that he might give us himself!

The fact is that we are a composite of needs. We are born into need as infants. Childhood needs turn into adolescent needs. Some needs change while others remain constant from birth to death. Each successive stage of our lives only reveals more needs. And before you sigh with a resigning whine, may I remind you of the words of our text! "My God shall supply all your need." That makes the matter of your needs and mine GOOD NEWS! God can only meet needs! He cannot do a thing for you at the point of your sufficiency or surplus! Men are lost and bound for hell today because of their supposed sufficiency, and will never be saved until there comes an overwhelming sense of need. Saved people are living without urgency or commitment because like the Laodicean church, they are saying, "We have need of nothing!"

A word of warning should serve well here. In identifying needs for the claiming of God's supply, it is wise to pass a matter through several gates before qualifying it as a need. It is easy to elevate our wants into needs and desires into necessities in this surfeited century of ours.

As we walk our prospective need through proper gates, let us first enter the gate of time. Let the matter soak and saturate in the element of *time*. You may discover it to be cared for within the context of right timing, and to have prayed for prior deliverance would have circumvented the processes of God. Let us next walk it through the gate of *thanksgiving*. Don't bother bringing a need to God unless first you have done the will of God regarding it. That is expressly stated in 1 Thessalonians 5:18: "In every thing give thanks: for this is the will of God in Christ Jesus concerning you." You may ask, "How can I give thanks for something for which I do not feel thankful?" That is precisely when you can do it best! Anyone can give thanks for something for which they feel deep gratitude. It takes faith to give thanks with an act of the will when the emotions are protesting with all their might. And remember that when you decide to do the thing God commanded, you have all his power supporting you in the doing of it. Next, let us walk through the gate of *importunity*. Importunity is simply the refusal to be denied. Importunity will either lead to the positive meeting of that need or will bring enrichment through the need.

A perfect illustration of this is in 2 Corinthians 12 concerning Paul's thorn. It must have been a continuingly grievous infirmity. He besought the Lord thrice regarding it, and as far as we know, it continued right through his life until his death. But he got an answer! His *obvious* need really was pointing to an *actual* need. What he thought he needed was the removal of the thorn. What God knew he needed was to trust God constantly, and the thorn was a constant reminder to drive him to that trust.

Now the obvious question, "Did God meet Paul's need?" Our text has already answered that, "My God shall supply all your need." The final gate to walk a matter through is the gate of *obtaining*. A statement from Alexander Maclaren needs to be held before us all: "The axiom of Christian faith is that whatever we do not obtain, we do not require."

It is easy in our culture to develop ideas of what we need for our comfort. Sociologists reported a few years ago that at the beginning of the twentieth century the average American wanted seventy-two things and considered eighteen of them important. Fifty years later the want list had risen to 496 of which ninety-six were considered necessary to happiness. It would not be hedging the truth to say that if our wants were met before they were sanctified into needs, the result would be catastrophic. It must be remembered that need is necessary, and God is interested in waiting until that need has had its necessary ministry in us before it is supplied.

ILLUSTRATIONS OF NEEDINESS

There were two common characteristics obvious in virtually all of the folks in the Bible who are held up as exemplifications of faith . . . they had reckoned on God as the source of all reality, and they had troubles and trials galore! Yet, they were folks who had moved into the realm of God's economy and found eternal answers. Listen to the record, "They were stoned, they were sawn asunder, were tempted, were slain with the sword: they wandered about in sheepskins and goatskins; being destitute, afflicted, tormented; (Of whom the world was not worthy:) they wandered in deserts, and in mountains, and in dens and caves of the earth. And these all, having obtained a good report through faith, received not the promise" (Heb. 11:37-39). These folks were living illustrations of neediness. Now could we say that their needs were not met? Not at all! In the midst of need, God was perfecting them. "God having provided some better thing for us, that they without us should not be made perfect" (Heb. 11:40).

Not only were their needs perfectly met, they were *perfected.*

Let us observe some of these who occupy faith's hall of fame. Take Abraham for instance. He had a God-given need. It was God, not Abraham, who had mentioned the covenant which would require a son. Abraham and Sarah lived past the normal child-bearing age, and the need continued. Their capacity to meet that need by normal human means was nonexistent. The need remained. In fact, it was rather urgent when analyzed in the light of human probability. Abraham graciously lived with need for a number of years, but not in desperation and frustration. "He staggered not at the promise of God through unbelief; but was strong in faith, giving glory to God; and being fully persuaded that, what he had promised, he was able also to perform" (Rom. 4:20-21).

And perform God did! And he did it in such a manner that he would receive all the glory. God can best crown with heaven's glory that which obviously has heaven's patent on it. Isaac was clearly a child of heaven. That is precisely the reason that when God called on Abraham to sacrifice Isaac, Abraham went without discussion or question. Abraham knew that Isaac was God's boy, and what God did with him was God's very own and exclusive business. And here is a vital lesson in the midst of met needs. When God does meet our needs, he is often obliged to detach us deliberately from the supply in order to keep us attached to himself. Our "Isaac's" must never be the occasion of detracting our affections from God himself. And if that happens, God will have us sacrifice our "Isaac" on the altar. Then he will meet the need brought about by our obedience. And God goes on creating needs and supplying them. He gives us Isaac's, commands us to sacrifice them, and then provides the ram caught in the thicket. And this continues on and on *ad infinitum* as God brings sons into glory!

Let's spend a moment with Moses. He was covered up in need. Some of the need was because he had not reckoned with God as the source of his total ability. He tried to do it himself by

killing the Egyptian. He spent forty years on the backside of
the desert living out the disaster of the work of the flesh. But
when the whole record was in, it read like this, "By faith Moses,
when he was come to years, refused to be called the son of
Pharaoh's daughter; choosing to suffer affliction with the people
of God, than to enjoy the pleasures of sin for a season; esteeming
the reproach of Christ greater riches than the treasures in Egypt,
for he had respect unto the recompense of the reward. By faith
he forsook Egypt, not fearing the wrath of the king; for he
endured, as seeing him who is invisible" (Heb. 11:24-27). Whatever his failures were when the final tabulations were in, Moses
was a winner! His life was a living illustration of need and the
abounding ability of God to meet every one.

INVITATIONS TO TRIUMPH

Your needs and mine are invitations to triumph. God has been
sending us such invitations down through the years of our lives.
Every invitation is marked RSVP. God wants a reply. The validity
of each such invitation depends upon our response. If we disregard
the invitation or refuse it by rebellion against need, no enlargement or blessing comes. This is one lesson that every triumphant
Christian must learn . . . that of properly responding to need
and adversity. If we do not learn this lesson, we will miss the
primary source of our enrichment and enlargement.

Jesus promised adversity, "In the world ye shall have tribulation" (John 16:33). James assumed adversity when he said,
"Count it all joy *when* [not if] ye fall into divers temptations"
(Jas. 1:2). Paul testified of trouble when he said, "But we glory
in tribulation" (Rom. 5:3). Then we need not be surprised or
taken with disappointment when what Jesus promised comes true
in our lives. We have somewhere developed a misconception
that if we are in the middle of the will of God troubles will
cease. This could not be farther from the truth. God is bringing
us into glory and we are reminded that "it became him [God],
. . . to make the captain of their salvation [Jesus] perfect through

sufferings" (Heb. 2:10). It is more than logical to assume that if our Savior were perfected by suffering, so may we be perfected. If he learned through all he suffered, so might we (Heb. 5:8).

One of the finest treatments of this matter I have ever read is found in a message by the late A. C. Dixon entitled "Through Night into Morning." Dr. Dixon, who served Moody Memorial Church and the Metropolitan Temple in London, observed:

> With some *Christians* it is winter—long nights with short days, much darkness and cold. With others it is summer—long days and short nights, with the bloom of flowers, and the song of birds, and beauty all about them. But with all Christians every night is followed by its morning, whether it be the long night of winter or the short night of summer. We want, first of all, to LOOK AT THE NIGHT, and then at the morning; to inquire what makes the night, and then what gives the morning. What is it that changes sadness into gladness, the gloom into the gleam? . . . As to *the night of calamities*, you can get a gleam, perhaps, from argument. John B. Gough said, when he went down to the Crystal Palace on his first visit to England, he was overwhelmed by the glory of the pyrotechnics. "It was a magnificent display," he said, "on a very dark night." But presently it all sank, the air was filled with bad odours, and he looked out upon gloom. "At that moment," he said, "I took a glance at the heavens, and there I saw the stars in their glory. I said, 'Thank God for His stars; there is no pyrotechnic display about them.'" There is greater glory in the stars than in fireworks. . . . The Lord Jesus Christ Himself, in any calamity, is more than argument. I have gone to see Christian people after they had lost their fortunes. One man of wealth, because of a new invention which spoiled his business, found himself reduced to poverty.

That man was not in the night: he was happy and
radiant, because he had a better consciousness of
Christ's presence. He said, "I never knew what it was
to have Jesus as all in all until I found myself reduced
almost to beggary, and began to count up my riches
in Christ. I was a millionaire in Him and did not know
it." He had to move down to a small, insignificant
street, but he took Christ with him, and he knew Him
better down there than he did on the Avenue in the
midst of wealth. . . . *The night makes the morning.*
The morning comes and drives away the night, it is
true, but God knows how to make the night produce
the morning. Jesus said, "Your sorrow shall be turned
into joy." Your Sorrow shall be transmuted into joy.
And certain it is that the darkness of Bedford Jail made
the morning dawn of *Pilgrim's Progress.* It was out of
that darkness of the jail the allegory came that has
gone over the world and down the ages. It was the
darkness of Wartburg Castle, into which Luther was
thrust, that made the light of the German translation
of the Bible. It is the darkness of Calvary, with its
broken heart and its sin-bearing, that makes the light
of salvation and of heaven. God knows how to make
the morning out of the night. He can touch the black
charcoal into diamonds. He knows how to speak and
the darkness becomes light. The very affliction that
would drag you down lifts you up; the things that are
weights become wings. That which, if you could, you
would have prevented lifts you up to heaven. . . .

In closing this discussion I want to make three suggestions
for your response to neediness and adversity:
First, *accept every circumstance and situation as a part of the
divine pattern of providence.* You can never do this on the basis
of your understanding or your ability to see clear through the

experience to light at the end. It will require faith in the faithfulness of God. Say, "This has happened to me through the will of God. That being true, it does not matter whether the devil did it or God did it. What really matters is my obedience to God in responding to the matter in order to be rendered redemptive. I receive the invitation, but there is yet another step."

Second, *give genuine thanksgiving and praise for the circumstance or situation.* We are not merely to tolerate a distasteful situation. We are to exult in it. Listen to these suggestions regarding neediness:

"*Be of good cheer;* I have overcome the world" (John 16:33).

"*Rejoice* and be exceeding glad; for great is your reward in heaven" (Matt. 5:12).

"Count it all *joy*" (Jas. 1:2).

"We *glory* in tribulations" (Rom. 5:3).

"Most gladly therefore will I rather glory in my infirmities. . . . Therefore, I take pleasure in infirmities, in reproaches, in necessities, in persecutions" "I will glory of the things which concern my infirmities" (2 Corinthians 12:9-10; 11:30).

"In every thing give thanks: for this is the will of God" (1 Thess. 5:18).

Do you have trouble in your mind obeying these clear instructions regarding need? Then let me ask you this: can you thank God for the cross? Of course you can! We sing about it and adore it with all its implication for our redemption and victory.

How can we love that vehicle of torture? Simply because in his power and providence, God was able to take the worst injustice ever perpetrated in the history of humanity and transform it to make it the best thing that ever happened. It has become the means of our redemption! If God can do that, he can surely take your circumstances and mine, and transform them through our obedience and praise into vehicles of redemption. Hallelujah for hardships! But there is yet another step.

Third, *hear the message God is speaking through the circumstance or situation, and implicitly obey.* It is easier to give thanks than to obey, but both are necessary. If we, like Christ, are to learn through all we suffer, we must obey in every matter until our obedience is complete.

In summary, our response to neediness should be: ACCEPT IT. PRAISE GOD FOR IT, AND OBEY!

A poem I recently read speaks volumes regarding this matter of needs:

> When God wants to drill a man
> And thrill a man
> And skill a man
> When God wants to mold a man
> To play the noblest part;
> When he yearns with all His heart
> To create so great and bold a man
> That all the world shall be amazed,
> Watch His methods, watch His ways!
> How He ruthlessly perfects
> Whom He royally elects!
> How He hammers him and hurts him
> Into trial shapes of clay which
> God only understands;
> While his tortured heart is crying
> And he lifts beseeching hands!
> How he bends but never breaks
> Whom his good He undertakes;
> How He uses whom He chooses,
> And with every purpose fuses him;
> And by every act induces him
> To try His splendour out!
> GOD KNOWS WHAT HE'S ABOUT
> AMEN!

13
BARRIERS TO THE MIRACLE

"And God saw every thing that he had made, and, behold, it was very good" (Gen. 1:31).

THE BEGINNING

When our world system began, there was one word to describe it—GOOD! *Good* is a good word . . . almost indefinable due to simplicity. If you have had an average day today, you have probably used the word *good* already more than once. If I were to ask you what it meant, you would likely say, "Well, that's what it means . . . good!" In *The Amplified Version* the words are added, "Suitable, pleasing, approved, fitting, admirable, sufficient, and satisfactory." Those are good descriptions of the system that God put into operation in the beginning. There was an abundance of everything—enough and to spare for everything. There was a flow of reality from God to the visible realm that was sufficient and beneficent. The whole creation, including man and woman, was a fantastically beautiful picture of an orderly operation.

The light was good. The sea and land were good. The vegetation was good. The sun, the moon, and stars were good. The fish and fowl were good. The living creatures on the earth were good. In fact, there are six times that the description is designated in Genesis 1. The earth was prepared for the crowning of creation. "Let us make man in our image, after our likeness: and let them have dominion" (Gen. 1:26). First, man himself was created and placed in the beauty of the garden. God said of him, "It is not good that man be alone; I will make him an help meet" (Gen.

2:18). It was not good for man to be as he was because in the state of being alone, he could not function to be all that God made him to be without woman. You know the story. God made woman from Adam's rib and gave her to Adam. Now he was complete! He had the capacity to be all that God had made him to become. That "was very good" (Gen. 1:31).

THE FALL

But the good was not to last. The sound of the voice of the serpent was soon heard in the garden. His advertisement was to the latent reason in the soul of the woman. In the hearing of the woman, the devil *doubted* the word of God, *denied* the power of God, and *distrusted* the motive of God. The three counts on which she fell are the same ones that the enemy is using today. She saw that it was good for food (lust of the flesh); that it was delightful to look at (lust of the eyes); and desired to make one wise (pride of life)—Gen. 3:6. She ate of the fruit and shared it with Adam. The result was the fall.

Could we know something of the vast and far-reaching implications of the fall, we would better appreciate the vastness of the gift of salvation in Christ. At this juncture, the significant observation is that of the effect of the fall on the total plan of God's economy in the world. Man forfeited his right to reign and handed it over to the devil. Man was no longer an *extension of divine presence;* he was an extension of a mere human presence, a fallen human at that. He was no longer an *expression of divine personality;* instead he was an expression of a selfish human being at best. At worst, he was the personification of the wicked ego of Satan. Man was no longer an *exhibit of divine dominion;* instead he was an exhibit of weak, sin-wrecked man.

It was no longer very good. It was not even a little good. It was bad. It was bad, because man's sin separated him from God. The flow of divine plentitude was broken. Man lost the capacity to communicate on God's level, and this meant he lost contact with reality in God. He now would live horizontally depending on what he saw and sensed to sustain and satisfy him. Reality was there, but man could not find it. His reason had overwhelmed his revelation. He had eaten of the wrong tree. He now would live by knowledge. God never intended this. God's will was that man live by revelation.

The plan of economy was still there, but lost man was living in disregard of it. His nature was foreign to it. That plan has remained until this day. The flow of plentitude is still there and anyone, anytime, under the proper circumstances can tap into it. Though a lost man can benefit from the general principles of the economy of God, he cannot himself get on the inside of the circle until that glorious operation called the new birth occurs, which equips him to be a man in two worlds. With the new birth, he is restored to the capacity of doing business in the realm of unseen realities where plenty reigns.

But even after a person is saved and the Holy Spirit comes to live in his being, there are barriers to the miracle of God's economy. It is sad to admit that even among the community of the redeemed, the percentage living in accord with the eternal plan of economy is small. There are barriers which could keep us from the plan for the rest of our lives. Let us expose these barriers and put them away. Let us view some of those barriers.

IGNORANCE

I find that there is a great hunger for spiritual reality all over the world. Folks are desiring—yes, even demanding—something more than vague promises of a future existence better than this. They are demanding a NOW salvation. This hunger is giving way to searching, and Bible teaching is springing up all over the land.

The scales of ignorance are falling from the eyes of the redeemed. The days of ignorance are at an end. The day of enlightenment has come. The world is hearing things about God's plan and provision that I never heard in my growing up days. Oh, if I could only have heard some of these truths. I wonder what my life might have been had someone told me of God's eternal, unchanging plan of economy. I gave for years out of a sense of duty—with everything but a joyful spirit. I floundered in shortages and insufficiencies for most of the first twenty years of my Christian life. I never heard a word about how to get in on God's plan of plenty. But one day I was informed!

STUPIDITY

I hesitate to use the word but after I have put it down I am glad . . . because this is exactly what it is . . . stupidity! When a man is ignorant and uninformed that is one thing. When ignorance is informed about the truth and does nothing about it . . . well, that is no longer ignorance but stupidity. It is stupid and foolish to refuse the best of life for a second- or third-rate plan. Once the message of this volume, or any part of it, becomes your information, you can no longer be ignorant.

GREED

The desire to have and keep is a strong drive within the human heart. The devil planted greed within the human heart, and it has robbed man of many riches. It is one of the greatest barriers to the miracle of God's economy. It is that driving greed that pulls back from giving all to God (in order to get into operation God's economy in our lives). The devil stirs up the greed in our hearts and says, "Don't give what you have. You earned it fair and square. If you give it, you will lose it!" Jesus says just the opposite, "Give, and it shall be given unto you" (Luke 6:38). The devil has reason on his side. It just doesn't make sense that when you give you get. It looks to us like when we give we lose. Two systems of truth strive for our response—visible and invisible. Too often the visible wins out. Greed governs. Selfishness is superior. Getting becomes the goal.

TRADITIONAL PHILOSOPHIES REGARDING ECONOMY

Some of the greatest barriers to the operation of God's plan of economy are to be found in prevailing present-day philosophies regarding economy. Let me just mention a few:

"Save for a rainy day." Now, while it is wise to keep in mind certain eventualities, it is not right to save as a preventative from having to have faith in God. A friend of mine has said, "If you are determined to save for a rainy day, be sure that there will be one sooner or later that will take all you have saved."

"The devil has most of the money in the world." It may appear that the devil and his crowd have all the vital financial holdings in the world, but I have news for you. God says, "I will give thee the treasures of darkness, and hidden riches of secret places, that thou mayest know that I, the Lord, which call thee by thy name, am the God of Israel" (Isa. 45:3). There is more wealth hidden away waiting to be possessed within the context of God's plan than we could ever imagine. In fact, that which seems to belong to the devil is in reality ours because it is God's. The Bible tells us that "the wealth of the sinner is laid up for the just" (Prov. 13:22). The wealth of this world and the next belongs to him who has all power. Power is wealth. No one is more wealthy in the final sense than is the totality of his power. The devil is a defeated foe, and all that he seems to possess is in his hand through an arrangement God has made. God is omnipotent, and with that power he possesses everything!

"Christians are supposed to be poor." You won't find this in the Bible. This is an idea that developed in the Dark Ages when the world was almost devoid of the Word of God. Men who did not know Jesus as The Truth sought to develop systems of their own. Poverty was a thing to be developed to make one "holy." Redemption, they thought and taught, was to be gained by personal sacrifice. This idea is foreign, not only to the Old Testament, but to the New Testament as well. Riches as an end in themselves are discouraged. We are enjoined to lay up treasures in heaven, not on the earth. But poverty is nowhere equated with righteousness. The believer is depicted as a "joint heir" with Jesus. All that is his is ours. We are as rich as he! Jesus always had enough. He seemed never to have a surplus, but he always had enough and was able to get whatever he needed anytime. That is true wealth! And this is the will of God for everyone of us.

"Save all the money you do not have to spend." We have previously mentioned the fact that there is a sore evil under the sun, namely riches kept by their owners to their hurt. While on the human side, hoarding makes sense, it is diametrically opposed to the principles of God's plan. A body of water dies when the flow is stopped. The Dead Sea is dead for one reason— there is no flow. Millions of gallons of water flow into it from the swiftly-moving Jordan, but the water dies, because it ceases to flow. This is true in any realm. You can kill a body by stopping the flow of energy. You can kill a church by stopping the flow of energy, loyalty, and money. We are to be channels, not reservoirs. We are to give, not hoard. A better adage for the day would be: "Give all that you do not have to spend." The world today is even recognizing the vitality of a principle which is opposite to the hoarding syndrome. Hence, all the incentives to buy, buy, buy to get money into circulation.

"When you need it, get it." Impulse spending abounds, and millions of people are in financial bondage because of it. The tragedy is that this bondage does not stop with finances. It spreads to the whole of one's life. Let me suggest that when you need it (and I mean really need it), believe God for it and give God an opportunity to get it for you to his glory. In this manner, God will be glorified, and you will be benefited.

Now these have been just a few of the old philosophies which have prevailed for a long time in our economy.

THE TITHE

This may come as a surprise to you, especially since we have mentioned the tithe as a good place to begin to recognize the ownership of God. But my friend, if you stop at the tithe, you have merely paid your debt. I want you to remember this adage:

TITHING IS A DEBT I OWE . . .

GIVING IS A SEED I SOW.

When a debt is paid, you cannot expect much from it. But when a seed is sown, you can expect a great harvest. We will talk of the matter of sowing toward a harvest later on.

The tithe was the minimum required under the law. Everyone is wise (even the lost) to the tithe. It is never profitable to rob God, and nontithers, lost and saved, are "God robbers." But to stop at the tithe is a barrier to the miracle of the operation of God's plan of economy. It takes giving God's way to get his grace into motion. When the giving stops, the flow clogs and the whole plan bogs down.

DEFERRED GIVING

Now, before you jump on this, let me say that deferred giving through wills, etc., is *one* way to give. But to resort to deferred giving *instead* of abounding in giving *now* is to build a barrier to the flow of God's plenty. I believe that every Christian should be concerned that the wealth he leaves behind be directed toward those endeavors which would glorify God. He should, thus, make arrangements for deferred giving. But don't let such arrangements prevent lavish giving *now!*

I just heard this statement a few days ago:

IF YOU'RE GIVIN' WHILE YOU'RE LIVIN',

YOU'RE KNOWIN' WHERE IT'S GOIN'.

The enterprising Christian should employ every advantage to the glory of God to get the wealth of this world invested in the souls of men through wills, insurance policies, trusts, etc., but any or all of these must not be taken as substitutes for giving of our means *now.*

PRAISELESSNESS

The absence of praise in any situation isolates that situation from the divine flow. It is praise that releases the power of God

into a situation. Thus, I say that praiselessness is a great barrier
to the miracle of God's economy. Praise is just a facet of God's
economy and represents the working of the whole system. As
long as there is a flow, there is soundness of economy.

I am writing this volume under the threat (of all things) of
financial pressure. I have never in my life had such repeated
assaults made upon my faith. I have just made a serious, life-
changing decision that has withdrawn everything from my account (literally and figuratively) and placed it at the disposal
of God. The devil seems to taunt me with the foolish things
I have done. When moments of restlessness come, I settle down
upon one foundation . . . I HAVE NOTHING FOR MYSELF
. . . IT IS ALL HIS . . . I AM IN HIS WILL, AND ALL HE
HAS IS MINE! Then I look not on the seen but on the unseen
and begin to praise the Lord! *Praise releases the true wealth
of God.* Doubt and complaining are barriers that block the flow
and lock up the wealth of God.

We have looked at only a few of the barriers that the enemy
uses to block the flow of God's wealth. It would be vain to
investigate them all. We need not know every approach of the
enemy if we will keep one rule in mind. *Believe that THE WORD
is the only adequate representation of reality.* Take God's Word
for it. The world has a system that is represented by volumes
of its best wisdom. The world system is crumbling now and is
destined for oblivion. Only the WORD OF GOD WILL STAND
FOREVER. What God has said to us is true wealth. God exalts
his Word because it is his means of getting truth into us that
will get us into him! He is a reality through his Word. We cannot
make evaluations by our common sense, our emotions, the con-
sensus of counselors, or anything else . . . only upon God's Word.

The devil does not know what to do with someone who is
set to believe the Word of God. The more you come to know
and apply the Word of God, the more your spirit will be
enlarged. The more the devil will fight you, and even this will
enlarge you. The greater the battle, the greater the victory, and

the cycle goes on. Even the devil is used of God to spur us to growth!

As we study the Word of God, we learn to believe God. When we learn to believe God without question, the devil is upset. We are a threat to his handiwork. The Word of God is a key to the operation of the principle of the laws of the spirit. The laws of the spirit govern the laws of the natural. Satan works in the natural world, and to employ the principles of the Word is to practice authority over the devil! When we learn the rules of the Word as operating principles in God's economy, Satan is a defeated foe!

Remove the barriers to God's plan, whatever they are. Move straight through the apparent to the real. Get through the nonrealities to the realities. Get stationed on God's Word. The plan is waiting for you! Get in!

14
REALITY REVISITED

*REALITY: That which is absolute; self-sufficient; not dependent
on anything else; ultimate as contrasted to the apparent.*

We have dealt with the question, "What is reality?" earlier
in the volume. Since that time I have been doing some more
thinking in the realm of reality and its importance to our relationship to God's plan of economy. I have looked over the information in that early chapter and have decided against making
any additions or revisions. In deference to that, I have chosen
to revisit the subject of reality with you here near the end of
the book. I am more decidedly convicted that your idea of reality
and mine will mean everything to our lives. What we believe
to be ultimate reality will determine where our final loyalties
and values lie.

Our primary question earlier was, "What is reality?" Our
answer was that God was the ground of all reality and what
we see and sense in the visible realm is temporary, while the
unseen is eternal (2 Cor. 4:18). Reality then is seen and sensed
only through the capacity of faith. But the question for now,
which seems more important as we come to the practical realms
of living, is, "What is reality to you in your daily living?" I want
to help you answer that question by asking you some others I
have asked myself.

What turns you on? What turns you off? What saddens, sickens,

142

or satisfies you? In what areas do your motivations lie? Which affects your life the most, the seen or the unseen? Which has more influence on your life, your problems or God's power? In what or whom do you find your thrills? Whose approval do you most desire to have? Now, stop and look back at these questions and give yourself an answer. When you have finished, you will have answered the primary question of what reality is to you. The true definition of reality has not changed, but your judgment of what it is has shaped your life. Let me ask you if you are satisfied with your answers. Have you been living in the realm of solid reality? Or do the things of this life—the physical, the mundane, the temporal—have you almost down for the count? The question I want to ask myself and you is this, "Have you seriously reckoned with reality and are you reckoning with it now?"

I am prepared to say that I greatly fear that ninety percent of all Christians have never reckoned with reality. They have rather been arrested by nonrealities, run by nonrealities, or wrecked by nonrealities. Man's basic difficulty is that he has mistaken *time* for *eternity,* his *body* for his *soul,* and *himself* for *God.* Reality lies in the area of eternity, the soul, and God, while nonreality centers around time, man's body, and his self-interests.

The wreckage of nonreality is tragic. First, *people are perishing.* Men are lost because they have mistaken the identity of reality. They have concluded that the things of this life are to be given priority. Like the rich man in Luke (16:19-31) they are preoccupied with the nonrealities of material possessions. We have been arrested by the apparent and have forgotten the real. Second, *Christians are crippled.* As in the parable of the sower (Luke 8:5-15), the care of this world and the deceitfulness choke the Word, and a person becomes unfruitful. Believers forget that their lives are hid with Christ in God. They are unmindful of their citizenship in heaven. They lose sight of their position with Jesus in the heavenly places. The result is a crippled, paralyzed

Christian. Third, the *church is chained.* The church is the mystical body of Christ on earth. It is his means of expression and mobility. Just as the individual can be imprisoned by nonrealities, so can the church. The local, visible manifestation of the church is but a picture of the mystical body. The realities of that body are unseen, because the resources of that body are in God as he has revealed himself in Christ. If we are not careful, we will be dealing with nickels and noses instead of eternal verities. You say, "But we must have physical things, and numbers are inevitable, and committees seem to be with us!" That is right, but these must never be allowed to dictate to the eternal realities or to overwhelm them. If that happens, we will be bound to the world's way of doing things, the world's plan of economy, and the world's power. The result will be that Christ will be shut out of his own church!

VIEWING REALITY

It is difficult to talk of reality without seeming vague and unreal. One reason for this is that we have dealt with the visible for so long that we consider anything invisible to be unreal. We view reality only when we are determined to do it. We must want to see in order to be able to see. We have been equipped with eyes of the soul to view reality, but we have so long kept those closed that it will take a while to get accustomed to the new view. This chapter began with a dictionary definition of reality. It is that which is absolute, self-existent, not dependent on anything else. That simple statement rules out everything we can see as being reality. Everything that we can see is passing away. The world system is deteriorating. Built within the system of things is the aging process. We are in the midst of change, and frankly, I see none that is on the upward swing. I can't find much to encourage me on the earthly scene.

> My hope is built on nothing less
> Than Jesus' blood and righteousness;

I dare not trust the sweetest frame,
But wholly lean on Jesus' Name.
EDWARD MOTE

If God and all that issues from him is reality, then we must not stop at defining reality—I must declare reality. Somehow, our confession at this point seems all-important. "If thou shalt confess with thy mouth the Lord Jesus, and shalt believe in thine heart that God hath raised him from the dead, thou shalt be saved" (Rom. 10:9-10). This is how confession brings reality. Faith is substance and evidence. State the fact that you refuse to build your existence on nonreality. Confess that you are choosing to make God the source of your supply. Declare yourself to reckon with reality!

VALUING REALITY

The greatest showcase which exhibits reality's value is Hebrews 11. One has to admit that here is a list of folks who had it all together! They knew how to live. And the inspired writer said one thing that really startles me more than anything else. He stated that these were people of whom the *world was not worthy* (v. 38). Here were folks who took the worst and licked it. They lived life to the hilt. They rendered the future present. They were surely accused of living in nonreality, but they had a firm grip through faith on eternal realities. The one thing we must admit about this crowd of people: *whatever they had really worked!* We know what they had: the roots of their faith had gone down to bedrock and struck reality, and they would not be swayed by deprivation or death. They had gotten the report of faith, and nothing would deter them from their goal. They were on their way to another world and were living in that world right in the middle of this world. Notice what is said of them: "These all died in faith, not having received the promises . . . " (Heb. 11:13). When we read that, we are prone to pity them because they didn't find what they were looking for. But let us see the rest. " . . . but having seen them afar off, and were persuaded of them, and embraced them, and confessed that they were strangers and pilgrims on the earth." Hallelujah! Do you see what I see? These folks took the long view of faith, and with the reach of that faith embraced things that we are enjoying this very day, and went out in victory! Their faith connected them with realities that were not yet visible in history but were as real to them then as they are now. The closing statement of Hebrews 11 is interesting. "These also, one and all, are commemorated for their faith; and yet they did not enter upon the promised inheritance, because, with us in mind, God had made a better plan, that only in company with us should they reach perfection" (Heb. 11:39-40, NEB). Doubtlessly we will all conclude that it was worth the wait!

When we awaken to the value of reality, we will not mind facing the loss of what we cannot keep to gain, that which we cannot lose. In the light of reality's value, all other value systems will straighten out. When we see the "pearl of great price," we will not mind selling all in order to buy that pearl. There will be the expulsive power of a new affection. God in us by Christ, through the Holy Spirit, will simplify our living and singularize our commitments. Our confession then can be, "I have discovered such a reality that it has captured my whole being. It wakes me up and puts me to bed. He (God revealed in Christ by the Holy Spirit) is my pearl of great price. Since I have discovered him and he has discovered me, all else has taken its place as significant only as it is related to him."

VALIDATING REALITY

I am going to deal with this later in the chapter on becoming a hilarious giver. But for now I will give you a solidly biblical formula for validating reality. We can know what reality is and value it highly, but unless we know how to validate it in life's circumstances, it will be to no avail. We have stated that true prosperity is the capacity to get God active with his supply in the needs of humanity. The psalmist gives us perhaps the simplest statement on validating reality. He said in Psalm 37:5, "Commit thy way unto the Lord; trust also in him; and he shall bring it to pass." Let us examine that statement.

"Commit thy way unto the Lord." There can be no validation of reality without commitment. A man may have a million dollars in the bank, but if he does not make a commitment to believe that and launch out on the truth of it and draw on his account, he might as well be a pauper. The commitment of one's way is a total commitment of one's self. The whole affair of life is to be surrendered to the Lord. That is foundational, primary, and fundamental. There is no need for further discussion until this is done. I have had times, and some of them recently, when thousands of issues seem to scream for attention in my brain. Peace only comes when I say, "Lord, these are not mine, because I am not mine. I confess that I have committed myself and all these issues to you." The only things that we need worry about are those things which have not been committed to God. And when worry over something that we have committed to him attacks us again we simply need to say, "Lord, I have committed this matter to you and believe your Word."

"Trust also in him." If we are not careful, we will find ourselves breaking down in faith after our commitment. Having committed our way to the Lord, we sometimes are prone to pray ourselves out of faith. The trust is as vital to *continuation* as the commitment is to *commencement*. Faith to commit must become faith to trust. If the answer does not come in visible terms it makes no difference. Our trust is in faith, not sight. We are satisfied with faith because faith is substance. Man often says, "Seeing is believing." The opposite is true. Believing is seeing. And when we see through the eyes of believing, those things we see are such solid stuff that this world can never take them away. Now, these two things are man's part: committing and trusting. You can be sure that if you have done this, something terrific is in the offing.

"He shall bring it to pass." The original implies simply, "He works!" He does it! Now we see one thing clearly. It is that man's activity has one peculiar significance . . . to move God into activity. There is nothing sacramental about man's commitment or man's trust, but they trust right through to reality and the result is that GOD WORKS! All man's work for God is simply that God might work. Notice this in the Bible. Noah's ark was built that God might work in the judgment of the flood. Moses' work in delivering the people, building the tabernacle, and leading them toward the promised land was that God might work in their behalf. Elijah's work on the altar and subsequent prayer were for the purpose of getting God back into the nations's history. These men *validated* reality and *visualized* reality!

Would you dare to validate reality in your own life? You will never come to reckon with reality until you are willing to release your grip on all the nonrealities. That is what it means when we "commit our way." We are to commit all our going and all that goes with it. Our trust keeps the commitment current. The result: GOD WILL DO IT! Whatever needs to be done, God will do it!

Our commitment and trust will have thrown into operation all the resources of divine reality into our circumstances. That will continue as long as we dare to validate eternal realities by continued commitment and trust.

A final word of exhortation: That commitment is seldom, if ever, so vague that you have nothing particular in mind. Usually there is an issue which points up the whole commitment. What we usually say in a commitment is that this particular thing has been a point of conflict in my relationship with God and I now release it along with all else to his care. It may be a savings account, a relationship with another person, a position, a gift, or any one of a myriad of things. Though the commitment is total, the issue is specific. "I will obey the Lord in this specific matter."

15
THE LAW OF THE HARVEST

"But this I say, He which soweth sparingly shall reap also sparingly; and he which soweth bountifully shall reap also bountifully" (2 Cor. 9:6).

In any realm there are certain inexorable laws which elevate the one who obeys them and applies them, and lowers and destroys him who violates them. There is no use to quibble with the law or seek to bargain for a change. Being a law, it is rigid. In our temporal plane there are certain laws that we are careful to keep. In the realm of the unseen and eternal, there are laws which are just as rigid and real as those by which we order our physical lives. Knowing the law and cooperating with the law puts us in a position to be advantaged by all its implications.

Meet the seed. What a remarkable little item! They come in all shapes and sizes and all have one thing in common: they have an amazing indwelling quality called life. *There is perhaps no system that so clearly depicts God's plan of economy as that which surrounds the law of the harvest.*

I grew up on the farm. Seedtime and harvest are no strangers to me. My dad was one of the finest farmers in our part of the country. I will give you his secret in a moment. Let us look at the seed. There is nothing quite like a seed. Man can make something that looks like a seed, but man cannot make a seed. He can manufacture something that will pass for a seed, and you would easily mistake it for a seed. But there is one quality always lacking in the man-made commodity—the inner-life system. Every seed has within it a life system exclusively peculiar to its kind. The seed knows nothing and hears nothing and yet

149

given the opportunity will obey to perfection the system of life which indwells it. It will never make a mistake but will always reproduce its likeness.

There is another thing about the seed that is vital to our observation. The life that is in it is imprisoned within it until certain conditions prevail, under which that life bursts into the open and releases the power of its life system. You can shine it and enshrine it, extol it and enthrone it, hallow it and hoard it, but until you cooperate with its inner-life principles, it is as dead as a door knob. You can place it on the mantle and so beautify it that folks gasp when they look upon it, but it is dead for all practical purposes. You can encase it in plastic and put it on a necklace and strike up a dozen conversations a day about it, but it cannot minister life. You can have lively conversations about it, but there is no ministry of life. THE SEED MUST BE SOWN!

How was my dad such a good farmer? Well, the fact of the matter is the *he learned to cooperate with the inner-life system of the seed.* He knew when to sow and under what conditions. He knew how to cooperate with the growth patterns of that particular seed and its life system right on through until the harvest. I never tired of watching the life systems of the seeds and my dad's cooperation with them. The result was always a harvest in proportion to the seed sown.

Every seed is a sermon in miniature. If that seed could preach and we would be willing to listen, our whole life-style would take on new dimensions of abundance. I was continually amazed at the infinite capacities of one little seed. A grain of corn about the size of the fingernail on my little finger would grow into a plant over six feet high! So much from so little!

Paul was speaking in 2 Corinthians 8 and 9 on the subject of giving. Right in the midst of this discourse he dropped in the *law of the harvest.* He seems to use the words *give* and *sow* interchangably. Giving is sowing. If we could see this, we should be living gloriously in God's plan of abundance. God's plan depends on the life system which he set in motion in creation, a life system that has never been killed out. The life within the seed is a picture of the life of God in every living thing on the earth. It is a picture of the larger life of God.

But what does it mean to *sow* the seed? Essentially, sowing the seed is to lose it, to bury it, to give it away. The seed which becomes fruitful is *obedient unto death, ceases to exist as an individual entity,* and *gives way to a larger life.*

Listen to John 12:24:

"Verily, verily I say unto you, Except a corn of wheat fall into the ground and die, it abideth alone: but if it die, it bringeth forth much fruit."

That little seed, a miniature picture of the great, wide kingdom of God, is placed in the ground alone and forsaken! And yet at this point the law of the harvest begins its operation! It is precisely at the point of the planting that the great law begins to function. Strange things begin to happen within the body of that little seed. It begins to respond to its environment in the cool and fertile ground by first swelling, then bursting. Its walls actually break apart. It can no longer hold the expanding life system . . . a system which begins to expand miraculously when the conditions are right. It swells, then bursts, and then sends roots down. At the same time, it sends shoots up. Obeying an order of life, it continues to obey to exactness certain unwritten laws right on through to the harvest when the returns are manifold. One grain of corn can grow a stalk from which as many as two or three thousand grains just like itself are produced. Amazing! One little, unassuming grain of corn, and yet it contains that much life.

In John 12:24 the obvious thing is that Jesus was not giving a lesson on farming, but on redemption. He was taking a familiar point of reference and illustrating a higher form of life. He was in fact talking of himself as the seed that would be sown. He was committed to death and was laid in a cold, dark tomb, much like the little seed is laid down in the cold earth. And the life of God in Christ burst forth in death and the result was life for millions of us. The seed (Jesus) was planted and God gave a great harvest—millions and millions of those who have life in them because of him.

Giving, whatever its nature, is an investment. It was so with Jesus. He made an investment of his life and is still reaping the dividends of that investment! The law of the harvest simply stated is—sow sparingly, reap sparingly; sow bountifully, reap bountifully! That law is working in your life and mine right now and will continue to work, regardless of what we think about it. It is working in us to wealth if we are obeying it, or to poverty if we are violating it. And every one of us is doing one or the other.

Again it seems wise to remind ourselves that we are speaking in a circle so wide as to include every commodity of life. This would involve such items as time, respect, love, concern, energy, as well as money. The law is always operative regardless of the commodity. If you are not reaping as you desire to reap, check on your sowing. Many people who have not experienced a seed-time have the audacity to expect a harvest! If you sow nothing, you can expect a harvest of nothing. A million times nothing is still nothing!

I want to break the statement of this law into three parts: *We always reap* what *we sow; we always reap* more than *we sow; and we always reap* later than *we sow.*

REAPING WHAT WE SOW

This is the law of likeness. If you sow weeds you are going to get a harvest of weeds. If you sow thistle seed, you will get a thistle bush every time. It will never fail. You can sow a million seeds, and you will always invariably get the same thing that was sown. The quality of that which is sown is bound inextricably to the quality of that which is reaped. There is locked-in likeness which guarantees against variation.

Likewise, this works well in the spiritual realm. You and I, like the seed, have an indwelling life system dominating us. Being put in circumstances which bring us to the death of our own plans for the commencement of his, we experience the bursting forth of the nature of that inner-life system. If that system within which dominates us is of the devil or of ourselves, then the life of God within us is violated, suppressed, imprisoned. When we consent to be planted to his glory so as to be exhibits of his indwelling life, the life he planted within us bursts forth.

In the same vein when we give, we will get in return the same quality. We will get *what* we sow. If we sowed discord, we will reap a bumper crop. If we sowed love, we can expect an abundant return. If we sowed respect, we can expect to be showered with it. We reap *what* we sow.

REAPING MORE THAN WE SOW

A part of the law of the harvest is that of multiplication. This is what makes it profitable. There would be no future in sowing if from the sowing we did not reap a harvest greater than the quantity of seed sown. It is a law written within the framework of the universe. *Sow a little, reap a lot.*

I remember that seedtime was to me the season of greatest intrigue. We were practicing faith of the highest order. We were putting thousands of tiny seeds in the ground, covering them, and expecting a harvest! There was more to getting the job done than driving the tractor and looking straight ahead. We had always to look in several directions almost at the same time. We had to keep an eye on the row so we would not get out of line. We had to watch the seed hopper lest its mechanism would fail or we would run out of precious seed. We had to watch the spout to see that the seed was flowing in. We had to watch the subsoiler as it plowed its little furrow to contain the seed. We had to watch for the telltale sight of tiny seeds to be sure that, when the covering device piled the fresh dirt around them, they would grow!

Sometimes as a lad I failed and forgot to watch. Just as sure as this happened, the spout would stop up, and down the row a quarter of a mile I would catch on—but too late! And, you know, a few months later when we harvested the crop it was still evident that I had not sown. There was a hauntingly vacant space in the field where I had failed to sow. All the cultivating that we did served to no purpose in compensating for the failure to sow. Where nothing had been sown, nothing was reaped. But where something was sown, something was reaped. And it was always much more.

As I write this, I am wishing that I might have taken the time down through the years to keep a record of the proportion of seedtime sowing and harvest. As I look back to those days on the farm, I am thinking of blackeyed peas, corn, wheat, maize, watermelons, cantelopes. I am wondering just how many hundreds, and in some cases how many thousands, of seeds came from one tiny seed! It is more amazing right now to me than it has ever been. This law of the harvest is operative, not only in the physical world, but in the spiritual world. The physical is only a picture of the real, the spiritual. If sowing in the physical realm reaps rich dividends, then why not in the spiritual? This is a world where everything is in unity. There is not a secular and a spiritual realm. God controls it all, and the seen is just a visible picture of the vast unseen world. We have already seen that "the invisible things of him from the creation of the world are clearly seen, *being understood by the things that are made,* even his eternal power and Godhead" (Rom. 1:20).

REAPING LATER THAN YOU SOW

I soon learned something as I came to the age where I could be a productive helper on the farm. The nature of the life within the seed included a time-processing system. This could be co-operated with but not circumvented. We simply had to respect it and go along with it, respecting its laws. Some matured from seed to full harvest size in ninety days and some in more time, but the harvest was always later than the sowing.

We didn't wait to see the harvest until we sowed. We knew that if we did not sow, there would be no harvest. At best, we could learn how to so perfectly cooperate with the seed life as to encourage full growth. The more we learned about the nature of the particular life system, the better we could cooperate with it to produce a greater harvest.

So, in the spiritual realm there is a life system waiting to burst out upon our world. It is in us and includes all the commodities which have been entrusted to us. When we begin to cooperate to the fullest possible degree with that system of life, fantastic things begin to happen. The harvest always comes later and abundantly!

CONCLUSION

We have authority from our text in 2 Corinthians 9:8 to believe that our giving is sowing. And if it is sowing, we can expect a harvest. A harvest will mean multiplication and plentitude.

For the sake of God's glory, let us be sure that we remember that we will reap *what* we sow without any variation. Therefore, let us sow that which we want most to reap! "Be not deceived; God is not mocked: for *whatsoever* a man soweth, that shall he also reap. For he that soweth to the flesh shall of the flesh reap corruption; but he that soweth to the Spirit shall of the Spirit reap life everlasting" (Gal. 6:7-8).

Don't forget, either, that we will reap much *more* than we sow. For heaven's sake (and earth's), let us not sow that which we do not want multiplied. All that this world needs, it needs much! A little will not do. Love by addition is not enough. It will take multiplication to meet the demand. Let us then sow love! And so with concern, esteem, kindness, and money!

And time is a factor! Thus we are enjoined, "And let us not be weary in well doing: *for in due season we shall reap, if we faint not*" (Gal. 6:9).

Would you get in on God's plan of economy. Go to the seed and be wise. There is a system of life all around you and within you waiting to be released. At the very moment when you begin to cooperate with the nature of this life, there will be abundance.

You don't understand it? Don't try to figure it out. I am not sure that anyone on our farm including Dad could have written a treatise on how one little seed could multiply its kind a thousandfold, or how many could be planted and yield a barn full. But we planted, anyway, and reaped a harvest! Our understanding was beside the point. The harvest of plenty was point enough. In fact I don't ever remember regretting my ignorance as to how it happened. I was too busy taking in the harvest!

Our responsibility is to sow. What happens after that is in accord with the power behind the life system. We are merely the sowers. God is the multiplier.

I can guarantee you on the authority of the Word of God that when you begin to sow, you will begin to reap. What do you most need? Begin to sow it. This will work in any realm. Happy sowing!

16
BECOMING A HILARIOUS GIVER

"God loveth a cheerful giver" (2 Cor. 9:7).

I have said repeatedly that giving is a key to the realm of God's economy. There is a right way and a wrong way to give. In our text Paul makes a simple declaration, "God loveth a cheerful giver!" My first response is, "Doesn't God love everybody?" As a matter of fact, he does. Then why would Paul say that? I know of only one solid, unimpeachable reason—he was inspired of God to say it! There might be other opinions, but I feel satisfyingly safe in this one! If God inspired him to say it, there was only one reason why he inspired him to say it— because it is true! While God loves everybody, it is safe to assume that God has a special love for a giver who is cheerful in the doing of it.

The word in the Greek is *hilaros* which sounds almost like its English counterpart *hilarious*. We will refer to the cheerful giver from henceforth as a hilarious giver, one beside himself with glee. I don't think it would be possible for me to put down in words just what I think a hilarious giver really is. I wish I could draw you a picture. If I could, I would capture the look of uncontained delirium, electrifying enthusiasm, ecstatic expectation. I would picture a face on the edge of rapture, a countenance exploding with delight, and could sound be added, a voice crackling with inner triumph. The hilarious giver is one who is carried out of this world by the privilege of giving! Almost giddy, always gleesome, he has discovered that it really "is more blessed to give than to receive" (Acts 20:35).

But alas, where are the herds of hilarious givers? I think that the species has all but disappeared if there were ever a great crowd of them. If giving is a God-given privilege and is the means of getting into God's providential pattern, then we should be happy about it. I keep looking for a church somewhere that takes the offering with exciting expectation during that period which tends to be a dead period filled in by enough music to keep us from sensing the deadness of it. If ever there should be a spontaneous season of praise, it should be during the offering. David used this time to bless the Lord in the midst of the congregation. That was right after the people rejoiced, and David the king rejoiced with great joy. (The reason for their joy is obvious; we will discuss it later.) I wonder what spiritual forces are waiting to be released when we can stand before God as hilarious givers. I cannot help but feel that there is a pent-up river of blessed spiritual reality waiting to come rushing upon us as we enter joyfully into the glory of godly giving.

Let's talk first about some *problems which prevent hilarious giving.* Two problems are mentioned in our text. The words used are "grudgingly" and "of necessity." In the former, one gives, but not willingly. In the latter, one gives, but because he has to. No one who gives unwillingly can be a happy giver. Nor can anyone be cheerful who gives because he is pressed to.

Giving as one can afford it is a problem which prevents hilarious giving. This is never to be the gauge of Christian giving. This reckons on the horizontal and not the vertical. It is giving that does not make a demand on God's ability and, thus, does not invite God to move into it.

Another problem in this realm is that of *giving until it hurts.* Folks who have given until it hurts just continue to hurt. That hurt is just a fraction from resentment. Hilarity isn't apt to break out in such a relationship.

Giving according to need is everything but hilarious. If we are prone to set our giving according to the need, there will soon be a time that our resources are exhausted. Need is never the final call to give. It may be what drives us to God to find our direction in giving, but need-oriented giving breeds spiritual pride and crass pity. The apparent need may be what aroused you to the necessity of giving, but don't stop there. When God has gotten your attention, however he first got it, let him set the gauge of your giving.

Giving on an emotional impulse also prevents hilarious giving. Just as sure as you become involved in a warm and exciting service and the offering is taken by someone who knows how to excite the human heart over giving, you may respond impulsively to a stimulus outside the Lord. Later on you will have a tendency to say, "What a fool I have been!" Then you will find ways to retreat from your commitment made in such haste. There is an infinite difference in Spirit-directed giving and impulsive giving. The Holy Spirit never pushes. He always leads.

Let us, next, view some *perspectives which promote hilarious giving*. Perspective is almost everything when viewing a situation. I will never forget when I began to see how this matter of giving could be hilarious. As I asked the Lord about a specific amount for a major gift to our church, I was so busy talking that God could not impress me with a figure. When I was quiet for long enough he did give me a figure. It was so big that I was almost sorry that I had been quiet! The more I thought about it, the more distressed I got. Then, finally I realized that the amount that the Lord had impressed me with was so large that it was impossible. If it were impossible, it was absurd for me to expect that I could do it. I began to chuckle about the absurdity of the whole affair. I think I got a glimpse of what it might mean to be a hilarious giver. My family and I made our commitment, knowing that it was impossible, but having a word from him to go on. What was impossible and absurd now became hilarious!

Here are some powerful perspectives!

God has a sufficiency of everything and is doing everything he can to get his sufficiency into our circumstances.

All God's sufficiency belongs to us for the benefit of spreading his word.

God will give us anything that we will use to glorify him. He knows that our needs must be met and so he ministers bread for our food (2 Cor. 9:10).

The more we give, the more there will be to give. This is the way God's system works. What he expects, he enables. *The Amplified Bible* translates 2 Corinthians 9:8 like this: "And God is able to make all grace (every favor and earthly blessing) come to you in abundance, so that you may always and under all circumstances and whatever the need, be self-sufficient . . . possessing enough to require no aid or support and furnished in abundance for every good and charitable donation."

We cannot ever outgive God, but it sure is fun to attempt it! God doesn't want us to give because he is broke. He wants us to give because we are!

So let's take our stand right here this side of God's unlimited resources and view the needs of this wide world with the knowledge that we can be the means, the channels of getting his supply to the suffering masses. He becomes the source, and we become the channels! That could become hilarious!

Next, let us investigate some *practices which perfect hilarious giving.* The old adage "practice makes perfect" is appropriate in giving as well. One of the most often-heard and least-heeded commands of the Scriptures is the command to rejoice. There is a little secret here that will be of help to you. Rejoicing is not an emotion at first; it is a decision. The emotion of joy is a result of the decision to rejoice. *Yes, you can decide to rejoice by faith when there is not one reason to be seen to rejoice.* We have already examined the command of James, "Count it all joy when ye fall into divers temptations" (1:2). Paul said, "Finally, my brethren, rejoice in the Lord" and again, "Rejoice in the Lord alway: and again I say, Rejoice" (Phil. 3:1; 4:4).

Next, may I suggest that you *make a daily practice of giving something away which you highly treasure.* I have found a principle that operates in the possession of things. When something that I enjoy very much becomes an end in itself and takes my attention from God, it is time to give it away more freely than before. That can apply to time as well as all other of life's commodities.

Again, when you have an opportunity or a call to give of anything, *preface it with a doxology of praise.* How praise perfects hilarious giving! Just say, "Lord, it is by your good, great hand that I have the privilege and the power to give after this manner. I praise you for this rich privilege. To be blessed is a blessing, but to be a blessing is a blessing *indeed.*" W. W. How got the idea when he wrote:

We give thee but Thine own, Whate'er the gift may be;
All that we have is Thine alone, A trust, O Lord, from Thee.
May we Thy bounties thus as stewards true receive,
And gladly, as Thou blessest us, To Thee our first fruits
*   give.*
And we believe Thy word, Though dim our faith may be;
Whate'er for Thine we do, O Lord, We do it unto Thee."

When in doubt, give! It is seldom the wrong thing to do; if ever there were a chance that you made a mistake in giving too much, God would surely deliver you from serious consequences. How God must delight in sending angels to give escort of protection to hilarious givers. They need protection. They may die of sheer joy!

When self rises against giving, exhort it! Rees Howell, that great intercessor of a recent generation, talked about his first lesson in "princely giving." He said later: "Since my money now belongs to the New Tenant, the old tenant has to be impartial about the amount he gives. The New Tenant by his nature is more generous than the old one; the latter has lived so long in Egypt and later in the wilderness under the law, that he has only been used at best to giving the tithe; so when the New Tenant wants to give princely gifts, He first tests the reality of surrender; if it is proved genuine, then there will be no future conflicts when large amounts are called for."

Practice giving anonymously at least some of the time. Every now and then, there is a need to make a gift of time or energy, love or money, when there will never be a cause for anyone's knowing who made the gift. There is a special sense of pleasure and hilarity in an anonymous gift! Try it!

When you are overdrawn in your account in a certain commodity, try giving that commodity to somebody. For instance, when discouraged, try cheering someone up. When you feel unappreciated, find someone and tell him how much you appreciate him. When you are physically drained, do something for someone which demands physical energy. When you are pressed for time, spend some time on the needs of a friend.

Finally, let us peruse some *products that prevail in hilarious giving.* It will do just to list some products that are on view when giving as giving should be. These are some words that are noted in 2 Corinthians 8 and 9:

Abundance of joy (2 Cor. 8:2).

Fellowship of ministering (2 Cor. 8:4).

Abounding in faith, knowledge, utterance, diligence, and love (2 Cor. 8:7).

Bountifulness (2 Cor. 9:11).

Thanksgiving unto God (2 Cor. 9:12).

There are three specific products of proper giving visible in these chapters. First, *love was exemplified.* Second, *the people were edified* through equality. Third, *God was glorified.* "They glorify God for your professed subjection unto the gospel of Christ, and for your liberal distribution unto them and unto all men" (2 Cor. 9:13).

I want to be a hilarious giver! I want to ditch the problems which prevent it, declare the perspectives which promote it, perform the practices that perfect it, and enjoy the products which prevail in it.

God makes us hilarious givers!

17
GETTING IN ON THE PLAN

"Therefore, my brothers, I implore you by God's mercy to offer your very selves to him; a living sacrifice, dedicated and fit for his acceptance, the worship offered by mind and heart. Adapt yourselves no longer to the pattern of this present world, but let your minds be remade and your whole nature thus transformed. Then you will be able to discern the will of God, and to know what is good, acceptable, and perfect" (Rom. 12:1-2, NEB).

I am trusting the Lord to have worked such a work of grace in you by now that your next question will be: "Great! Where do I sign?" And we have come to that! For the precepts are ultimately no more powerful than is the practice of them. We have been amply warned against listening and stopping there: "Only be sure that you act on the message and do not merely listen; for that would be to mislead yourselves. A man who listens to the message but never acts upon it is like one who looks in a mirror at the face nature gave him. He glances at himself and goes away, and at once forgets what he looked like" (Jas. 1:22-24, NEB).

I am going to make four simple suggestions of how you can get in on God's miraculous plan of economy:

ONE: *ENTRUST THE TOTALITY OF YOUR SELF AND YOUR POSSESSIONS TO THE LORD.* Now, before you reply, "Why, I did that a long time ago!," let me suggest that you carry through some practical implementation. Get a tablet of paper and begin to list every asset you possess, beginning with your own body and its strength, abilities, gifts, etc. List your children, parents, wife, husband, and friends. Put down the amounts in your checking and savings accounts, bonds, stocks, and other investments. List your achievements that have recommended you to usefulness in your field. Put down your degrees and honors

won. List your home, automobiles, retirement pay, insurance policies, and trusts. Put down your furniture, your pets, your stor-
age of groceries, and your prospects of advancement at work.

List your pastimes, hobbies, plans for vacations, and things
you anticipate doing the most. These are your riches just as much
as your savings account. Don't forget the value of a good credit
line, the advantage of a good name in the community, and the
esteem of a great number of friends. Don't pass over that ability
to win friends, or make a good speech, or preach a good sermon.
That is included in your possessions. Count in your capacity to
care, to love, to feel the needs of others. Count that poise and
air of calmness when others are in panic. Put it all down! List
every friend you feel that you could not do well without.

Do you have everything down? When you have, write across
the pages in big, bold letters: NONE MINE, ALL HIS! Can
you really mean that? Don't go through the motions until you
do! God may come calling for any one of these things at any
time. And if they are truly his, you will not have a word to
say about his taking them from you and doing with them what
he pleases.

My family and I recently made a world tour, visiting our
mission fields and preaching to our missionaries in Southeast Asia,
Israel, and Spain. We came back with the world on our hearts
and a determination to do anything that it took to make our
hearts consistent with our concern. My spirit began to be in
turmoil. I looked at my own expanding ministry, its physical
and financial demands, and began to feel that my needs were
far greater than my supply in every realm.

I was committed to God as far as I knew. I had given the
possession of everything to him. I reminded him of that. There
was still no peace. I was in a struggle with God. I didn't mean
to struggle, but it was there. Desperation came, and in the midst
of that dark desperation, I cried one afternoon at my bedside
on my knees, "Lord, I have nothing—it is all yours!" Suddenly
the words *all yours* were more significant than all the rest . . .

all yours. I had again committed the possession of all that I was and had to him. I am convinced that we need to reiterate this at intervals whenever he suggests. If not, our hands will get sticky, and we will begin to hold too tightly those things which have come to us in the graciousness of God. I was free! Free from bondage, yes, but free also from blessings. For the greatest of his blessings can become curses when they turn our hands from him!

Having reckoned him as the sole possessor of all you formerly held title to, you are now ready for the next step.

TWO: *RECKON UPON GOD AS YOUR TOTAL RESOURCE, REFUSING EVERY HORIZONTAL SOURCE AS A FINAL MEANS OF SUPPLY.* As you reckon thus, you not only have the advantage of all that you gave to him, but all that he has which is yours in Christ. When you let go of all you had, you became the possessor of the riches of Christ in the "heavenlies." When you became available in all that you were to him, be became available in all that he was to you! Praise the Lord! Now, confess it out loud: *"My God is now supplying all my need according to his riches in glory by Christ Jesus."* That is truth from God's Word! You have chosen to transfer that truth into reality by your confession. Keep on confessing it! God has never failed to keep his word—not once! Stand on it! It is solid ground! Peter found it as firm as the "pavement" under his feet when he stepped out of the boat. And so will you!

And if that last statement has become a bother to you, remember that every *horizontal* source became God's property, along with everything else. Thus, you can refuse every horizontal source as a final means of your supply. If your job became the Lord's, then the salary you make comes from him as he allows you to keep his job. God, not your employer, is your source of financial supply. God, not your family, is your source of love. God, not your abilities, is the source of your confidence. God, not anything or everything else, is all you need! Say to him:

I need Thee ev'ry hour, Most gracious Lord;
No tender voice like Thine, Can peace afford.
I need Thee ev'ry hour, Stay thou nearby;
Temptations lose their pow'r When Thou art nigh.
I need Thee ev'ry hour, In joy or pain;
Come quickly and abide, Or life is vain.
I need Thee every hour, Most Holy One;
O make me Thine indeed, Thou blessed Son.
I need Thee, O I need Thee; Every hour I need Thee!
O bless me now, my Saviour, I come to Thee.

ANNIE S. HAWKS

THREE: *BEGIN TO GIVE FROM YOUR NEW SUPPLY SOURCE, ASKING FOR A WORD ABOUT WHERE TO BEGIN RIGHT NOW!* You may be facing an opportunity to invest in God's cause right now. That investment may involve talents, time, energy, gifts, relationships, material possessions, or anything else. The easiest place to begin is in the area of money or material possessions. Don't overlook this as unimportant. Usually the financial picture is an index to the whole of the spiritual life. If things are not right here, they are not right anywhere! I am going to make a suggestion concerning two places where you might ask the Lord about beginning your giving. First, in an area of *surplus.* Then, second, in an area of *shortage.*

Let's discuss the *surplus* area. You have an area of giftedness where you are never uncomfortable. You have plenty of whatever gives you confidence in this area. This may be where you need to make a solid gift. Why? God can't meet a surplus, only needs. If you have been so strong for so long in that particular area, you may have been that long away from his power in that area! In responding to God's mind in this area, you will experience a shift in confidence from yourself to himself. I suppose that I must give an illustration of what I mean. Suppose you have the gift of making money. That is one area you can fall back upon again and again and feel competent. You may need to give at the point of a monetary surplus to be able to trust the Lord instead of yourself. Ask him what he desires you to do in this area.

Now, let's discuss the *shortage* area. Remember, Jesus said, "Give, and it shall be given unto you" (Luke 6:38). If there is a shortage, God is having to work in your behalf to keep his supplies from reaching you. There is a reason, and you should find it. It is likely in the point of your giving. The basic principle in the Bible is *give unto abundance but hoard unto poverty.* Insufficient income is often caused by inadequate giving. You may have choked the income flow by choking down the outgo flow. Get a word from God and give.

FOUR: *EXPECT GOD TO WORK IN HIS BEHALF IN YOUR CIRCUMSTANCES IN AN OBVIOUS FASHION.* Believe that he desires this for you and claim it from him. He wants to invade your circumstances and bring you into such adjustment to him that your relationship will be something special. Learn to believe his word and his promises, and do not try to protect his reputation by rationalizing the promises. When the Word makes a promise, try it out without a doubt. Jesus said, "I tell you, then, whatever you ask for in prayer, believe that you have received it and it will be yours" (Mark 11:24, NEB). Don't try to explain that verse—just believe it! Try it out in a specific point of your life today. You have put up with a matter in your life far past the point of propriety. You have allowed the enemy to harass you long enough. Take the Word of God to be literal. Expect a miracle—a divine intervention today. Believe it now and stand on the certainty of your faith without having to have visible confirmations to strengthen your faith.

Now, in conclusion let us go through the checklist again: Check beside the declaration when you have done it:

_____ 1. I have entrusted the totality of myself and my possessions to the lord.

_____ 2. I now reckon upon God as my total resource, refusing every horizontal source as a final means of supply.

_____ 3. I now choose to begin to give from my new supply, and ask God here and now to give me positive direction.

_____ 4. I expect God to work in his behalf in my circumstances in an obvious fashion.

A Commitment to Commence

I, _____, do here and now affirm that from this moment on, the government of my affairs, possessions, and circumstances will be upon His shoulders. I choose that Jesus Christ and he alone will be the Lord of my life. "Have thine own way, Lord! Have thine own way! Hold o'er my being Absolute sway! Fill with thy Spirit Till all shall see Christ only, always, Living in me." I choose your total plan for my life. I am no longer my own, but thine. Put me to what thou wilt; rank me with whom thou wilt; put me to doing, put me to suffering; let me be employed by thee or laid aside for thee, exalted for thee or brought low for thee; let me be full, let me be empty; let me have all things, let me have nothing; I FREELY AND HEARTILY YIELD ALL THINGS TO THY PLEASURE AND DISPOSAL.

This is my commitment (or recommitment) to commence with him!

Signed_____ Date_____

Place_____

I AM IMPRESSED THAT THE LORD DESIRES ME TO DO THE FOLLOWING AS INDICATIVE OF THE GENUINE- NESS OF MY COMMITMENT:

1. _____
2. _____
3. _____
4. _____
5. _____